T0079708

LEMON

Edible

Series Editor: Andrew F. Smith

EDIBLE is a revolutionary new series of books dedicated to food and drink that explores the rich history of cuisine. Each book reveals the global history and culture of one type of food or beverage.

Already published

Apple Erika Janik

Bread William Rubel

Cake Nicola Humble

Caviar Nichola Fletcher

Champagne Becky Sue Epstein

Cheese Andrew Dalby

Chocolate Sarah Moss
and Alexander Badenoch

Cocktails Joseph M. Carlin

Curry Colleen Taylor Sen

Dates Nawal Nasrallah

Gin Lesley Jacobs Solmonson

Hamburger Andrew F. Smith

Herbs Gary Allen

Hot Dog Bruce Kraig

Ice Cream Laura B. Weiss

Lobster Elisabeth Townsend

Milk Hannah Velten

Olive Fabrizia Lanza

Pancake Ken Albala

Pie Janet Clarkson

Pizza Carol Helstosky

Pork Katharine M. Rogers

Potato Andrew F. Smith

Pudding Jeri Quinzio

Rum Richard Foss

Sandwich Bee Wilson

Soup Janet Clarkson

Spices Fred Czarra

Tea Helen Saberi

Vodka Patricia Herlihy

Whiskey Kevin R. Kosar

Lemon

A Global History

Toby Sonneman

REAKTION BOOKS

Published by Reaktion Books Ltd
33 Great Sutton Street
London EC1V ODX, UK
www.reaktionbooks.co.uk

First published 2012

Printed and bound in China by Eurasia

British Library Cataloguing in Publication Data
Sonneman, Toby F., 1949–
Lemon: a global history. – (Edible)
1. Lemon. 2. Lemon – History. 3. Cooking (Lemons)
I. Title II. Series
641.3´4334-DC23

ISBN 978 1 78023 034 4

Contents

Introduction:
A Fragrance of Lemons

> If I were forced to give up every fruit in the world
> but one I would have absolutely no trouble choosing.
> The lemon wins, hands down.
> Laurie Colwin, *More Home Cooking*

A decade ago, I would have been mystified by the quotation above. I love fruit – raspberries, peaches, pears, plums, apricots, apples, mangoes and more – but I would never have chosen lemon as my favourite.

Then, in an effort to discover what foods triggered my disabling migraines, I tried eliminating many common foods, including citrus, from my diet. I was shocked to discover the one food I missed most of all: lemon. Without realizing it, I'd been squeezing lemon juice on salads, fish and vegetables, and adding zest to baked goods. On my lemon-deficient diet, everything tasted a little blander, lacking that lively acid note.

I was so relieved to discover I had no adverse reaction to lemons that I wanted to run to the grocery store and buy bags of them, fill every bowl in my house with them, make fresh lemonade and lemon meringue pie, walk through lemon orchards and learn all I could about lemons. Living without

Lemons, which originated in India, now grow in subtropical areas around the world.

lemons, even for a short time, had given me a blossoming new appreciation. I would never take them for granted again.

As I examined the lemon's history, I discovered I had more than a passing acquaintance with its ancestor, the citron, an essential symbol of the Jewish autumn harvest festival. This fruit was so important to my ancestors that when my grandmother emigrated from Russia to America in 1913, she brought a special oval silver container used only during the seven-day festival to keep the citron fresh. After the holiday she made preserves from citron peel to give to new mothers, including my own mother, in the folk belief that it would restore their strength.

Besides drawing from my family history and the many books I read, I also absorbed the lemon's story from places and people. In Sicily's Lemon Riviera I rode the little blue Zappalà & Torrisi bus between coastal villages, winding along a road bordered with lemon groves. I spent days at a working lemon orchard *agriturismo* and visited Sicilian cooking authority Eleonora Consoli, who generously shared her insights into the island's cuisine, history and love of lemons. 'A gust of citrus blossom perfume presses us to stop, to discover a small corner of paradise', she had written in a cookbook on citrus. On the island where lemon trees reign, this corner is never far away.

Far to the north of Italy, at the foot of the Alps, I visited restored lemon greenhouses from the seventeenth century and realized how miraculous fresh lemons must once have seemed to residents of northern countries. Southern Italy's Amalfi Coast is famous for lemons, but it wasn't until I'd climbed a spiral of stone steps around a steep hillside layered with lemon orchards, high above the Mediterranean, that I sensed the wonder of them. Ancient stone walls enclosed tiny

Golden Meyer and 'Pink Variegated' lemons together with the more common lemon (Eureka or Lisbon).

garden orchards perched on narrow terraces, each a tapestry of trellises, intertwined branches, leaves and large moon-yellow lemons, their fragrance infusing the air. Never had I experienced a landscape so exquisitely shaped by human hands, so ancient yet so alive.

Nearer to home for me, California's lemon orchards were no less marvellous. In a dozen journeys to Southern California, in tours of orchards, packing plants, processing facilities and a most memorable journey through the Citrus Variety Collection with Professor Emeritus W. P. Bitters, I absorbed all I could about the fascinating lemon.

For years now I've always had a bowl of lemons in my kitchen, and simply smelling the aromatic oils of lemon rind, I recall the happiness of walking through a Southern California orchard on a December day, embraced by the exhilarating fragrance of lemon trees, blossoms and fruit. The lemon's refreshing, restorative quality draws me back, time and again – as it has for people across the globe for centuries. Today, if I had to give up every fruit in the world but one, I would not hesitate to choose the lemon.

I
Origins and Obsessions

The first citrus trees grew long before there were people to eat their fruit, in a region extending from East Asia to Australia. About twenty million years ago, botanists say, when Asia and Australia were joined as one continent, the three naturally occurring wild species of citrus came into being: mandarin, pomelo and citron. All other forms of citrus we know today – orange, grapefruit, lemon, lime – are hybrids, ancient natural cross-breeds of these three.

Most of the lemon's genetic heritage comes from the citron, a fruit that often looks like a freakishly large, knobby lemon. In fact, visitors to Italy's fruit markets often mistake the citron for a jumbo lemon. But anyone planning to squeeze a citron for a tall glass of lemonade will be sorely disappointed in the dry, bitter nature of its flesh. The wonder of this fruit is not in its culinary value, but in its history as spiritual symbol – and object of religious obsession.

Travels in Antiquity

The citron probably originated as a wild species growing in northeast India. It is one of the earliest recorded citrus fruits,

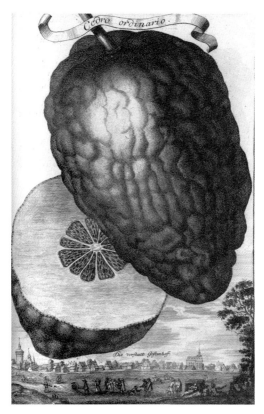

Cedro Ordinario,
or ordinary cit-
ron, from J. C.
Volkamer's
*Nürnbergische
Hesperides* (1708).

its seeds found in Mesopotamian excavations dating from
4000 BC. The earliest written reference to it is a Hindu religious
text from before 800 BC.

No one really knows how or why this fruit migrated from
India to Media, an ancient country that is now northwestern
Iran, then travelled south to Persia by 600 BC and on to
Babylonia, where exiled Jews discovered it and later transported it to Palestine. Alexander the Great's army, returning
from India to Macedonia around 300 BC, carried citrons to
the Mediterranean. The citron was the first citrus to be known

and cultivated in Europe, initiating a great flowering of citri-culture in the Mediterranean region.

The Greeks nicknamed the fruit 'Median apple' because it grew in Media, and this may be the origin of its botanical name, *Citrus medica*. However, its formal name, *kitrion*, is possibly derived from *kedris*, or cedar cone, which the immature citron resembles in shape and colour. The Italian name, *cedro*, still reflects that connection, visual rather than botanical, to cedar. In Latin the word *citron* was extended to the entire family of trees collectively known as citrus. Later, French, German, Polish Czech, Slovak and Scandinavian languages adopted *citron* (or a similar word) as their name for lemon, causing a lot of linguistic confusion. It takes expert detectives to decipher whether 'citron' in historical documents refers to lemon or to citron. In English the name 'citron' does *not* refer to a lemon but to its primeval ancestor.

By any name, the citron was highly esteemed by ancient peoples. But just what *was* it that they found so appealing? Today we appreciate citrus for its flavour and juiciness, a result of its unique internal structure. As the fruit forms, the rind becomes thick and leathery, while the inside fills with small pulp sacs, clustered in segments and usually filled with juice. Even lemons, lacking all sweetness, are valued for their abundance of clean-tasting acidic liquid.

Not so the citron. Beneath its thick skin is a wide spongy layer of white tissue called the albedo – slightly sweet but uninspiring to the palate, though ancients sometimes used it in salads – and a small wheel of pale green pulp, studded with little seeds. The seedy flesh is dry and its acidic flavour has an unpleasant bitter edge. In short, it is not good to eat. Theophrastus, the Greek philosopher and father of botany, succinctly captured this quality. 'Its fruit is not edible,' he wrote of the citron, 'but it has an exquisite odour.'

This drawing of *c.* 1646 by Leonardi Vincenzo, from the collection of the 17th-century natural scientist Cassiano dal Pozzo, shows the citron's thick albedo, the white inner tissue. While the citron's pulp is dry, bitter and inedible, the albedo is slightly sweet.

Over the centuries, only one significant exception to citron's inedible status has emerged: candied citron rind, a fundamental flavour in Italian panettone and English fruit-cake. This treat developed in the fifteenth century when citron peels were soaked in seawater for 40 days before being submerged in a sugar solution. Today the bulk of citrons grown for candying comes from Puerto Rico, where the fruit is fermented in concrete vats for three months before being de-pulped, chopped into tiny cubes and shipped in wooden barrels filled with salt- and sulphide-laced water. Confectioners, mostly in Holland and Germany, desalt the fruit, boil it and saturate it in a concentrated sugar syrup.[1] As for unadulterated, fresh citrons, there is virtually no market for them anywhere in the world.

Yet despite the citron's nearly inedible quality, the ancients treasured it. Both Theophrastus and the Roman naturalist Pliny the Elder, nearly 400 years later, considered citron an antidote to poison and a medicine for a great variety of maladies. It was said to cure snakebite, seasickness, dysentery, muscular pain, gout, stomach aches and coughs. Physicians prescribed citron flowers to relieve shortness of breath, crushed citron seeds mixed with wine as a laxative, and all parts of the citron to promote sweetness of breath.

Above all, citron was valued for its scent, that 'exquisite odour'. Citrus rind is pitted with tiny glands containing aromatic essential oils, and nearly all citrus oils smell good. But the citron's fragrance is particularly so, a concentrated lemon-and-lime aroma that evokes both floral sweetness and citrusy freshness in one breath. Citron's greatest attraction really is skin deep.

This marvellous oil – 'possessed of the most wonderful properties', as one botanist wrote – became a sought-after luxury, the fragrance of royalty and affluence. In Roman times, when citrons adorned the bridal chamber, it was also a perfume of love.[2]

Botanists in antiquity offered a number of labour-intensive methods to extract the oil. One instructed the collector to rub cotton wool saturated in sesame oil onto citrons as they grew – three times a day for 40 days. After these 120 rubbings, the perfumer picked the fruit and gently scraped the oil from the rind with a small silver spoon. Such painstaking work suggests that citron-scented oil must have been more precious than gold.

A Sacred Fruit

Indeed, in antiquity the citron was considered priceless, for its fragrance evoked the divine. 'The fruit seems always to have had a curious connection with magic and religion', writes Alan Davidson in *The Oxford Companion to Food*.[3] Hindus depicted the god of wealth, Kuvera, holding a citron, a symbol of prosperity. Jews adopted it as an essential part of religious practice. After the fruit reached China in the fourth century, Buddhists embraced the Buddha's Hand citron, an eccentric variety which splits along the length into a number of their finger-like lobes, so named because when the finger-segments press together, the fruit resembles a hand in prayer. In China and Japan, Buddha's Hand citrons were (and still are) cherished as religious offerings for household or temple altars. Their scent is said to evoke happiness. And in the seventh century Islam's prophet Mohammed chose the citron as a metaphor of true faith, saying, 'A believer who recites the Qur'an is like a citron whose fragrance is sweet and whose taste is sweet.'

For ancient Jews the citron took on a wholly different dimension. It was more than a representation of prosperity,

Unknown artist, *Fingered Citron*, *c.* 1822–40. The Buddha's Hand citron was grown in China from the 4th century. Buddhists in China and Japan use them as religious offerings in household and temple altars.

The Jewish harvest festival of Sukkot requires a *lulav* (a palm branch bound with myrtle and willow branches) and a citron (*etrog*), which together are essential symbols for the holiday blessing.

happiness or even spirituality. It was a fragrance that travelled wherever they went, a golden image shining on coins, a distinctive symbol of identity.

An agricultural people in biblical times, Jews considered their harvest festival, Sukkot, the year's most important holiday, so significant that it was known simply as the 'festival'. Other peoples had harvest celebrations, of course, but what distinguished the Jewish holiday was the citron – known by its Hebrew name, *etrog* – which fulfilled the Torah's commandment to 'take the fruit of a goodly tree', along with three types of branches (called the *lulav*). These became essential symbols in the central blessing of the holiday, which commemorates the 40 years that Jews wandered in the desert after the Exodus from Egypt.

Uprooted, in exile, the Hebrews designated the citron as a tangible natural representative for a people and their persistence, their wanderings and their resilience. They required fresh, unblemished citrons to fulfil the biblical commandment each autumn, and so they became citron farmers, cultivating the trees wherever they travelled. After the fall of Jerusalem in AD 70, exiled Jews dispersed through the Roman Empire and planted some of the world's earliest citrus orchards. In this way, the tree took root in Spain, North Africa, Asia Minor, the Aegean, Greece and Italy. In effect, the Jews' annual desire for citrons – a basic market demand with a religious twist – sparked the great Mediterranean citrus culture, which later blossomed under Arab influence.

For centuries, Jews who lived far from subtropical or Mediterranean citrus-growing climates had to pay exorbitant prices to obtain perfect unblemished citrons grown to exacting specifications – and so a lucrative trade sprang up. Merchants, savvy to what the market would bear, travelled from Austria, Germany and Poland to select the best fruit, often paying outrageous fees for royal or ducal charters. Yet no matter what the cost, sea travel was uncertain and riddled with dangers. Would the citrons arrive in time for the holiday? Would they meet the strict requirements for ritual use? Would there be money enough to afford the best? Anxiety was a seasonal condition for Jews in cold climates awaiting ships carrying the specially grown citrons from Italy, Spain, Corsica, Corfu, or (after 1850) Palestine.[4]

If fortune, fate and financial incentive converged to deliver a citron that both met ritual standards and arrived in time for the Sukkot holiday, a family cared for it with affectionate reverence, nestling it inside a finely crafted box of silver or wood, on a thick cushion of silky flax to protect it and prevent it from drying out. The citron was treated as royalty, like 'a diamond or rare gemstone or a cherished heir-loom which has been entrusted for safekeeping', Sholom Aleichem wrote, 'as precious as life itself . . . tenderly swaddled in flax, as one would a delicate child'.[5] Each morning of the holiday, when the box was opened and the citron removed for prayer, a heavenly fragrance filled the air.

Traditionally, after the holiday was over, the citron was retired from its ritual role and turned over to the women for secular use. Folk wisdom determined the citron's special relationship to women, and a variety of Old World post-holiday practices connected it to pregnancy and birth. A childless woman who wanted a son was advised to bite the tip of the fruit. A woman in labour could ease the pain of childbirth by placing the tip of a citron under her pillow. A pregnant woman who ate the citron after the holiday, according to the Talmud, would give birth to a 'fragrant' child – the equivalent of a 'good' child. Women soaked citron peel for days to decrease its bitterness and made it into marmalade, saving the golden preserves to give to postpartum mothers, as it was said to help them recover strength after childbirth.[6]

'Shameful and foolish, making such a fuss over a lemon', wrote a fourth-century Christian bishop, disparaging the Jewish fervour for the citron (and confusing it with the lemon).[7] By then the Jews' centuries-old connection with the fruit was in full flower. Although barbarian invasions had destroyed much of Europe's citrus cultivation by the end of the fourth century, some citron orchards remained in Southern Italy, Sicily and Spain, most likely because the citron was not only essential to religious practice but also a distinctive symbol of a people. And while religious faith had sparked the spread of citrus to Europe, economic incentives ensured it would continue.

Heritage

Over the last few centuries, even as Sukkot's importance has diminished for many Jews, Orthodox Jewish communities faithfully cling to the strictest traditions, each family selecting the most ideal *etrog* they can afford. Because a ritual citron cannot have any blemishes, scars, splits, insect damage, discolouration or missing parts, a top-of-the-line premium citron, by the refined standards of ultra-Orthodox Jewry, becomes the most expensive fruit on earth for a few days, and can sell for hundreds of dollars.

Cultivation of ritual citrons, guided by heritage and a search for perfection, is not only highly lucrative but also highly demanding. Since a sixteenth-century rabbinic decree prohibited grafting *etrog* trees onto stronger, disease-resistant rootstocks, the trees are short-lived, vulnerable to disease and frost. Traditionally, honeycomb-like cells of wood trellis support the trees and the entire orchard is covered with protective netting. Every stage of the growing, picking and packing process is labour-intensive to remove imperfect specimens and carefully nurture promising ones.

Today most citrons for the Jewish ritual market are grown in Israel, with smaller numbers grown in Italy, the Greek islands, Morocco and Yemen and, more recently, California.

'Farming citrons is so intense, it boggles the mind', says John Kirkpatrick, who started growing citrons for the Jewish holiday in California's San Joaquin Valley in the 1980s. Through the summer growing season, trusted workers painstakingly inspect the fruit, using small mirrors and magnifying glasses to examine the hidden side of each developing citron for scars or blemishes. They slip small transparent nylon bags around each fruit to shield them from insects, sunburn and wind scuffs, and secure the bags to branches.

A postcard published in Poland around 1910 shows Mediterranean Jews picking citrons for the Sukkot holiday. The text, in Yiddish, reads 'In an *etrog* garden.'

אין א אתרוגים-גארטען.

Of the 100,000 immature citrons in John Kirkpatrick's orchard, only about 12,000 will be cultivated to full size, and many of those will be rejected in the sorting and grading process, leaving just 2,000 to 4,000 that are good enough to sell during the short and manic market season defined by the Jewish lunar calendar. From one day to the next the fruit's value plummets, from being highly profitable in the few weeks before Sukkot to nearly worthless after the holiday begins. A Yiddish phrase to describe something of no value is 'an *etrog* after Sukkot'.

In small, intense pockets around the world, the growing, selling and buying of ritual citrons for a Jewish holiday can seem as much obsession as observance. Yet some 2,000 years ago, when the Jewish people chose the citron as a sacred fruit and launched this trade, they also helped establish citrus culture in the Mediterranean, from which arose the lemon's unpredictable journey through the secular world.

2
Sicily: Arab Mediterranean

Where, when and how did the lemon travel before it came to the Mediterranean? Tracing a precise route and timeline is nearly impossible. The lemon, an ancient natural hybrid, can also hybridize easily and produce spontaneous mutations. That makes it difficult to discern whether references or depictions represent citrons, lemons or some mixture of the two. Further complicating the history are the many, often interchangeable, names for citrus fruits.

But one thing is certain: more than 1,400 years ago, Muslim Arabs fell in love with the lemon in India and Persia. They swept the fruit along with them wherever they went, filling gardens and courtyards in Spain, Sicily and North Africa with the scent of citrus blossoms as they sowed the seeds of an agricultural revolution.

The Arabic name for lemon, *laimun*, glides off the tongue like honey, and in the soft caress of consonants and vowels you can hear the Arabs' romance with the fruit that the Persians called *limoo*. The desert warriors who burst forth from the Arabian Peninsula in the seventh century not only conquered vast expanses of territory but also consumed the wisdom of such advanced societies as Persia. Ravenous for knowledge of science, medicine, philosophy, agriculture and the arts, the Arabs absorbed a dazzling culture of learning and carried it westwards to the Mediterranean, launching a golden age in the midst of Europe's so-called Dark Ages, especially in Spain and Sicily. And along the way, they planted lemon trees.

A Garden Paradise

The Persians, who grew flourishing citrus gardens, took great pleasure in the lemon, from its leaves and wood to its flowers, fruit and rind. From them the Arabs learned to preserve the fruit in brine, make it into syrups and candy, and squeeze its juice over meat and fish to marinate and season them. They shredded citrus twigs for toothbrushes and extracted essential oil from lemon rind for soaps and perfumes.

To Muslim Arabs the beauty and aroma of citrus suggested the Qur'an's Garden of Paradise; thus they celebrated the lemon and orange in poetry and learned to grow and care for the ornamental trees. The first known written reference to lemons is in an Arabic agricultural manual of AD 904 which distinguishes lemon from citron and explains that the *laimun* tree is very sensitive to cold.

Islamic expansion in the eighth and ninth centuries in turn extended citrus culture to Egypt, North Africa, Spain and Sicily. In Spain citrus trees adorned courtyards and gardens. Nineteen rows of sour orange trees bloomed and fruited in the courtyard of the Great Mosque of Córdoba. In Seville homes, courtyards were embellished with lemon, citron and sour orange trees. Grenada's Alhambra palaces, built in the mid-1300s for Spain's last Moorish rulers, displayed a lasting affection for decorative citrus, with gardens of lemon and orange trees encircling fountains.

A 17th-century Persian tile captures the Persians' love of lemons, no matter how small.

In the ninth century Islamic armies conquered Sicily, soon followed by farmers eager to plant the island's fertile soil. They brought with them a host of new crops from the East, including aubergines (eggplants), rice, watermelon, pistachios, sesame seeds, the hard wheat used in pasta, sugar and citrus – sour oranges (sweet ones took a different, and later, route into Europe) and lemons.

Most significantly, early Islamic farmers employed sophisticated agricultural techniques they had learned in India and Persia. These former desert dwellers regarded water as the earth's most precious resource and borrowed every irrigation device they encountered, particularly from Persia. They became world experts in water use, practicing a system of intensive cultivation that turned the island into a garden paradise.[1]

The lemon's part in the ancient miracle of irrigation is still evident in Sicily's Lemon Riviera, a lovely green swathe of orchards between the Ionian Sea and a flank of Mount Etna called the Timpa. The orchards here, climbing the hillside from the sea to the Timpa's steep plateau, still use irrigation systems that look very similar to those introduced by ninth-century Islamic farmers. Webs of irrigation canals, carved of lava stone, carry water through the orchards. At each juncture of two canals, the flow of water to a particular section can be controlled – started or stopped – by inserting or removing a stone tile.

Simple as this irrigation system may seem, it was enormously significant to Mediterranean agriculture – and to lemons. Sicily became the world's top producer and exporter of lemons for centuries (until California overtook production in the early twentieth century) and still supplies more than 90 per cent of Italy's lemons.

Lemons are an essential element in Sicily, not only of the landscape but also of the palate. Sicilians adore lemons. They

A century-old irrigation canal in a lemon orchard in Sicily is very
similar to irrigation systems brought to the island in the 9th century.
Borrowing and diffusing agricultural techniques they'd learned in India
and Persia, early Islamic farmers created an agricultural revolution in
the Mediterranean.

are known to pluck a lemon from a tree and bite right in, rind
and all. Or they might peel a lemon with a knife and eat the
sour flesh with simply a pinch of salt. Although lemons in
Sicily and southern Italy are slightly less acidic than most,
this practice, as Clifford Wright observes in *Cucina Paradiso*,
'would make most North Americans cringe'.[2] A popular Sicilian salad consisting of diced lemons, peel and all, dressed
simply with olive oil and salt, is only slightly less dramatic.
Innumerable Sicilian dishes with meat, chicken and fish employ
lemon as an indispensable ingredient, and many traditional
sweets, including granita, sorbet and gelato, feature lemon.

This affection for lemons, originating from the Arabs'
200-year sojourn on the island, was adopted by those who
followed. When Normans conquered Sicily from the Arabs

in the second half of the eleventh century, they inherited a garden paradise rich in agriculture, particularly citrus. Palermo had become a magnificent city under Arab rule, boasting countless mosques, parks, fountains, courtyards and pleasure gardens scented with citrus blossoms. A fertile valley called the Conca d'Oro (Golden Conch) opened like a great golden shell filled with orange and lemon groves.

The Normans in Sicily seemed oddly entranced by Islamic culture – except its religion – and incorporated many elements of its style. They dressed in flowing robes, kept harems, carried on scholarly discussions in Arabic, integrated Islamic design in architecture and adorned royal gardens with citrus trees. They also embraced Arab foods and cuisine, even employing Arab chefs in royal kitchens to cook for the kings. And many of those foods – again, strongly influenced by Persia – employed the Sour Principle, meaning that a sour element could invigorate food.

There is ample evidence that sour meat dishes were consumed in the early Middle Ages, and likely before then. A thirteenth-century Arabic cookbook offered recipes for sour meat dishes such as *limūniyya*, chicken cooked in lemon juice with onions, leeks, carrots and aubergine (eggplant). 'Take a hen, joint it and put it in the pot, then throw the vegetables in it', read the instructions. 'Take choicest lemon juice, strain from its sediment and its seeds, then throw it in the pot.' Crushed almonds, ginger, mint and rosewater were added to the dish, a variation of which was sweetened with sugar.[3]

In medieval Egypt Jews made 'lemon hen' for the Sabbath with chard, onions, safflower and green lemons.[4] A Sicilian version of the dish, which may have been cooked in the Normans' royal kitchens, combined chicken with lemon juice, capers, almonds and pistachios, all served in a hollowed-out loaf of bread.[5]

Picking lemons in a grove on the Conca d'Oro outside Palermo, Sicily, c. 1906.

Lemon is one of the most ubiquitous foods in Sicilian kitchens, notes Eleonora Consoli, a native Sicilian who is an authority on traditional cooking[6] – a result of the Arabs' profound influence, both directly, during their reign, and indirectly, from the rule of Normans and the 500-year rule of Arab-influenced Spain.

Lemon juice is essential in preparing artichokes, making lemon salad (served in hollowed-out lemons), cooking fruit jellies and for squeezing over sardines. 'Lemons exalt food', Consoli says. One recipe she offers, *polpette*, calls for wrapping meatball patties flavoured with lemon rind between two lemon leaves before grilling. It is a fragrant and delicious appetizer – and assumes there will always be a lemon tree nearby. For most Sicilians, this is not a problem.

Granita di limone

One cannot speak of Sicily and lemons without a mention of lemon granita, an intensely refreshing sweet-sour frozen confection of sugar mixed with water, lemon juice and rind. Sicilians' passion for granita is such that many eat granita even for breakfast, often accompanied by a soft roll called *brioscia*, or brioche. In a traditional cafe or bar, with or without brioche, in every season and at any time of day or night, waiters serve up elegant glass dishes with pale yellow scoops of the island's signature delight, *granita di limone*.

On Sicily's eastern side this passion is connected not only to the coast's prolific lemon groves but also to Europe's most active volcano, Mount Etna. Along with plumes of smoke and slow-moving lava flows, the mountain is known for its snow. Before refrigeration, snow provided an astonishing and invaluable source of cold in the relentless scorch of summer. In ancient times Greeks and Romans packed snow into caves on Etna's slopes and withdrew it as needed to chill their wine. Snow merchants profited from Etna's natural cold power into the 1940s, collecting snow from the grottos every night and hauling it in horse-drawn carts down the mountain to Catania, where it was used to preserve food and make ice cream.

The island's earliest Arab residents must certainly have employed Mount Etna's snow for their delicious slushy drink called *sarbat* or *sharbat*. A cold fruit-sugar syrup, it was consumed between courses to refresh the palate and likely evolved into the sweet ice we call sorbet or sherbet. Yet it is

Lemon is one of the most popular flavours of the frozen confection granita. Many Sicilians, especially on the eastern side of the island, eat granita for breakfast.

only legend that sorbet and gelato were born in Sicily during the Arab reign, since real ice cream was not made until the endothermic principle of putting salt on ice was introduced around 1650.[7] Granita, however, is not a true ice cream but a kind of frozen lemonade, and its origin is probably much older, enjoyed long before ice cream was invented. Lemons and sugar, both native to India and Persia, formed a natural marriage of sweet-tart tastes, and the most natural concoction one could make was simply to combine the two.

On Lemon, Its Drinking and Use

The earliest recorded lemon recipes were written in Arabic, in a twelfth-century Egyptian treatise. *On Lemon, Its Drinking and Use* is undoubtedly the longest-lasting homage to the lemon, a medical cookbook with health recommendations and recipes written by Ibn Jumay, an Arabic-speaking Jew who, like his colleague Maimonides, served as court physician to Saladin, the great Muslim leader.

Ibn Jumay was famous in his time, celebrated for saving a man from being buried alive. One day he had watched as a cloth-covered body, carried on a funeral bier, passed by his clinic. Noticing that the feet poking out from the cloth were not flat but upright, a sure sign of life, the physician realized the man was not dead but rather suffering from a cataleptic attack, a condition causing muscular rigidity and the appearance of death. He could be revived.

Although Ibn Jumay's reputation swelled after this event, it was already well established. He was chief of the medical college, an advocate for clinical training of medical students in hospitals and a scholar who read ancient works in the original Greek. He had authored important medical treatises such as *Direction for the Improvement of Souls and Bodies*, a compendium discussing medicines, diet, hygiene and therapies, which was consulted frequently in his day and beyond.

In contrast, Ibn Jumay's minor treatise, *On Lemon, Its Drinking and Use*, seems more like a little cookbook with health advice than a scholarly work. It contains various preparations of lemons for restoring health, and so many recipes for lemonade that Samuel Tolkowsky, in his classic volume on citrus, *Hesperides: A History of the Culture and Use of Citrus Fruits* (1938), called Ibn Jumay 'the theorist of the art and preparation and use of lemonades'.[8]

Ibn Jumay's method for making preserved lemons – slitting the fruit and filling the gashes with salt, then pressing them into a jar, covering with lemon juice and letting them ferment for weeks – is the first known published recipe for this food, and virtually the same method used by modern cooks. Bacteria and yeasts that develop in the fermentation process soften the rind of preserved lemons, changing the aroma from bright and sharp to rich and rounded.

In the Middle East and North Africa preserved lemons impart a fine perfume to distinctive savoury dishes. *The Link to the Beloved*, a thirteenth-century Arabic cookbook, suggests the popularity of preserved lemons with the comment: 'salty lemons are so well known they need no description'.[9]

Preserved lemons, as food scholar Charles Perry notes, represent a culinary speciality of a region stretching from India to Morocco. Moroccans call them 'lemons that have been put to sleep', but their intense exotic flavour awakens the taste buds. In India preserved lemons are pickled with lemon juice and strongly flavoured with spices such as ginger, cardamom or cayenne. Preserved lemons in Afghanistan are flavoured with black cumin seeds, while in Morocco and other parts of North Africa spices are rarely added. In Egypt and Syria lemons are rarely preserved in this way, but salted lemon slices, drained overnight and covered with oil, are eaten as pickles. In Moroccan stews or tagines, preserved lemons are often combined with olives and chicken or lamb.

Ibn Jumay also recommended lemon peel, which, he wrote, 'stimulates the appetite, assists digestion and perfumes the breath'. Lemon juice, he advised, was a remedy for everything from inflammations of the throat and tonsils to indigestion and headaches, from 'giddiness of bilious origin' to 'the intoxicating effects of wine'.[10]

Tancrede R. Dumas, *Lemonade Vendor and Customer*, 1860–1900. Lemonade has been enjoyed in the Middle East since at least the 12th century when the Egyptian physician Ibn Jumay published a treatise on lemons with dozens of recipes for lemonade.

Why was it that this minor treatise on lemons, with its recipes and folksy recommendations, survived for centuries? The answer lies in a vast translation project undertaken by Islamic scholars, beginning in the seventh century and continuing through the Middle Ages, in which hundreds of Greek medical, philosophical and scientific works were rendered into Arabic. In later years, these works of antiquity were translated from Arabic into Latin, preserving for posterity Greek scholarship, layered with Arabic commentary and interpretation.

On Lemon, Its Drinking and Use is an illustration of this process of translating and transforming knowledge over centuries and cultures. No manuscript of the treatise survived the twelfth century. Yet we know nearly everything Ibn Jumay wrote about the lemon more than 800 years ago, thanks to a great Arab botanist of the next century, and indirectly to a Greek physician and botanist of the first century AD.

Ibn al-Baitar, born in Islamic Spain in 1197, was from an early age fascinated by both botany and medicine. Beginning in his twenties, he travelled over a vast territory of North Africa, the Middle East and Asia Minor, collecting plants and books by botanists everywhere he went. He always carried with him scholarly texts on botany and medicinal plants, including the five-volume *De Materia Medica* (Regarding the Materials of Medicine), one of the most influential herbal books ever written.

De Materia Medica, which described 500 therapeutic plants, was written by Dioscorides, who had practiced medicine and botany in the Roman Empire in the first century and had also travelled widely, including to Greece, Crete and Egypt. Nearly 1,200 years after Dioscorides wrote his pharmacopeia, it inspired Ibn al-Baitar to write his own encyclopaedic *materia medica*, in Arabic. Later still, over the course of centuries, Ibn al-Baitar's volume was translated into Latin and repeatedly published in France and Italy. Latin translations, called *Dictionary of the Simple Remedies* or *Simplicibus*, were printed in 26 editions from the fifteenth century until 1758, and the text was used to develop the first London Pharmacopoeia issued by the College of Physicians in 1618.

Incorporated into Ibn al-Baitar's *materia medica* were all of Ibn Jumay's recipes for lemonade and preserved lemons – the entire text, in fact, of *On Lemon*. And accompanying the twelfth-century doctor's recipes and recommendations was the confident idea that lemons benefited both health and cuisine. Like the lemon itself, that idea quietly made its way through the centuries and into the fabric of European life.

3
Exotic Treasure

Dutch still-life painters adored lemons. Seventeenth-century artists such as Pieter Claesz and Willem Claesz. Heda painted hundreds of them, luminous renderings using multiple layers of vivid pigments and glazes. A whole lemon casts an ovoid of sunlight upon a pewter plate. Gleaming slices of lemon and cut lemon halves accompany fish, oysters and meat pies. Giant curls of lemon peel accompany wine-filled goblets, glasses and gilt cups.

Strikingly, the lemons in these paintings are always prominent, never insignificant. Placed in the foreground, painted with sensual delicacy and a kind of reverence, they cast a golden light close to the viewer, as if to seduce the gaze.

Today the lemon might seem ordinary, but in seventeenth-century Europe it was anything but. Starting in the late eleventh century, Crusaders had brought back citrus and other desirable goods from the East and in much of Europe lemons remained both costly and coveted for centuries. At a Westminster Hall banquet given for Henry VIII and Anne Boleyn in 1533, among the luxuries gracing the table was a single lemon, which had cost six silver pennies. Even in 1662, when a dozen 'unwasht' lemons could be purchased in a London market for three shillings, they were far beyond the reach of labourers, who earned only about a shilling a day.

By the 1600s, when the Dutch were enjoying their Golden Age, with supreme naval power and ships bringing treasured goods from around the world, exotic imported lemons were as utterly desirable as a silk tablecloth or Venetian wineglass. And capitalistic Dutch Protestants – the richest people in the seventeenth-century Western world – enjoyed flaunting their wealth, perhaps by ostentatiously displaying lemons on their banquet table. If a Dutch burgher could not often afford such perishable items as floral bouquets, sugary confections,

Still-life in the style of Willem Kalf (1619–1693). In the 17th century, the affluent bought paintings such as this to signify ostentation and wealth. A lemon, which was highly expensive and considered exotic and precious, is given prominent placement on the table.

exotic spices or lemons, he could still in a sense lay claim to these objects by displaying a still-life painting of them in his home. Tens of thousands of seventeenth-century still-lifes fulfilled just such desires.

Those who could afford lemons found spirited pleasure in the zest, a flavour so uplifting that in medieval times physicians prescribed it as an antidote for melancholy (the word 'zest' retains this association with lively enjoyment). The Dutch and Flemish often flavoured wine and spirits with lemon zest, much like today's citrus-flavoured vodkas and gins. Their still-life paintings captured this trend too, placing lemons near wine-filled goblets or glasses. Typically, the lemon is peeled to midpoint in a continuous ribbon still attached to the fruit, and often a twist of peel curls down the tablecloth, a coil of golden light.

Lemons also featured in the seventeenth-century fashion for edible decoration. 'Jagged lemons', round, notched slices of unpeeled fruit, garnished a whole fish, lobster or crab, a joint of mutton or a roast pigeon, quail or lark. Round 'lemmon' slices and lemon halves pricked with rosemary branches accessorized a 1638 'grand salad', alternating with quartered roasted eggs around the plate's rim. A French cookbook of 1652 suggested lemon salad, an arrangement of thinly sliced peeled lemons topped with sugar, orange and pomegranate blossoms. Pickled lemon peel brightened winter salads, such as 'A Sallet of Lemmon, Caveer [caviar], Anchovies, and other of that nature', advised by William Rabisha in *The Whole Body of Cookery Dissected*, published in London in 1661, 'to corroborate the palate, and cause appetite'.

The idea of a sweet 'after-course', considered an antidote to the banquet's overindulgence, was as yet confined to the wealthy. Expensive imported sugar, long associated with lemon, was still out of reach for ordinary people, and thus another symbol of opulence. The rich and royal adorned banquet tables with spectacular sugar-work and spun-sugar sculptures of castles, towers, knights, horses, bears and so on – to be both admired and consumed. Fruit jams or jellies, thickened with pectin from lemons, were also considered luxury desserts, served in elegant small dishes and eaten with a spoon. Citrus peel candied in sugar was imported from the Mediterranean to England in special containers, or made fresh from imported ingredients.

Oranges and lemons preserved in sugar syrup, a time-consuming but impressive technique introduced to Europe by the Arabs, became a staple of the English banquet, the fruits' rich colours beautifully displayed in Venetian glasses. By the eighteenth century, as exotic preserved fruits took more eccentric forms, sugar-syrup for lemons was coloured crimson with the insect-based dye cochineal. The sour yellow fruit became a sugary pink confection, the colour of candyfloss.[1]

In seventeenth-century Europe, however, it was still rare to see lemon used in sweet dishes. More frequently, it found a savoury place on banquet tables – as well as in Dutch banquet paintings – as an accompaniment to fish and shellfish, or an ingredient in poultry and meat dishes. The sour element, a basic principle of medieval cuisine inherited from the Arabs, recognized that the acid note could elevate foods as effectively as spices, awakening a dish from bland slumber. Vinegar and tart fruits or leaves, such as gooseberries and quinces, or verjuice, the juice of sour grapes, were staples of the seventeenth-century kitchen – and lemon juice admirably supplemented or replaced them. Gervase Markham's *The English Hus-wife*, a popular cookbook of 1615, for example, recommended verjuice to sharpen a broth that was too sweet, while a 'flat and wallowish' broth could be brightened or 'quickened' with oranges and lemons. The British enjoyed the

In this still-life, painted by Willem Claesz. Heda in 1634, the luminous lemon is positioned next to drinking vessels of silver, green glass and gilt, testifying to the luxuriousness of the lemon and the fashion for flavouring wine and spirits with lemon zest.

pickled lemons they had discovered in India, and began adding lemons to a wide range of seventeenth-century dishes, such as 'cullis' or coulis, a meat broth flavoured with bread crusts, herbs, lemon slices and lemon juice. Although verjuice and vinegar remained popular, trends favoured the milder, fresher taste of lemon juice – if one could afford the lemons.

The seventeenth-century lemon was still far from being the most important fruit for European cookery, as Alan Davidson described it in *The Oxford Companion to Food*.[2] But it was poised, as if on a pewter plate in a still-life painting, between decorative and essential, between savoury and sweet, between the kitchens of the wealthy and those of everyone else. European cooks were just beginning to recognize lemon as a vital ingredient, a treasure.

The Medici Family

When fourteen-year-old Catherine de' Medici arrived in France in 1533 to marry the king's son (who later became Henry II), she found the court still consuming heavily spiced medieval fare. Catherine was accompanied by a bevy of chefs and pastry cooks from Florence, who also brought Italian recipes. Their recipe for duck with orange sauce, for example, might have been a cousin of *limonia*, a dish of chicken cooked in lemon juice which appeared in Italian cookbooks as early as the thirteenth century.

It seems likely that Catherine's cooks had a role in promoting lemons and other citrus in France, for the Medici family had a passion for citrus that lasted for centuries. It began in the early 1400s, when Cosimo de' Medici grew citrus trees in

Cosimo III de' Medici commissioned Bartolomeo Bimbi to paint the 116 varieties of citrus in his garden. *Citrus Fruits,* painted in 1715, represents 34 labelled varieties. The rarest lemons and citrons, resulting from complicated crosses, appear in the bottom row.

giant pots, and continued with Francesco I de' Medici (1541–1587), Grand Duke of Tuscany and one of the world's earliest collectors of citrus trees. One of the Medici villas near Florence, Villa di Castello, was later renowned for its impressive collection of citrus and its vast *limonaia*, or lemon house, a grand light-filled building where lemon trees, each in a large pot with the Medici insignia, could be carried inside for protection in winter.

Grand Duke Cosimo III (1642–1723) cultivated 116 varieties of citrus in the Medici gardens. Four large botanical paintings by Bartolomeo Bimbi documented their stunning diversity, with numbered labels naming each variety. Fittingly, in the Renaissance oranges were sometimes called by the neo-Latin word *medici*, an etymological twisting of the Greeks' original name for citron, Median apple.

Orangeries: Glasshouses

Although fresh lemons and oranges were much loved in northern Europe, they were also highly expensive and difficult to import, so the idea of growing one's own citrus trees was very appealing. Visitors to Italy, inspired by beautifully designed Renaissance gardens and Tuscan ingenuity in wintering cold-sensitive trees indoors, came home to France, Germany, England or the Low Countries eager to plant exotic novelties such as pomegranate, lemon and orange trees. By the middle of the sixteenth century northern European horticultural markets carried on a brisk trade in citrus trees imported from Italy in balls of earth.

Of course, these subtropical trees had to be protected during northern winters. Oliver de Serres (1539–1619), a French garden expert, encouraged the fashion for citrus greenhouses

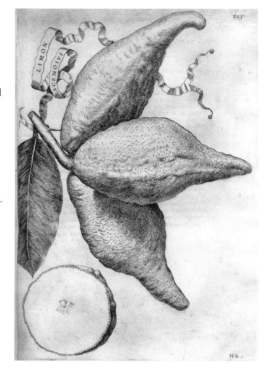

Aristocratic gardeners in the Italian Renaissance prized citrus mutations and strangely shaped fruits such as 'Limon Racemosus', likely a lemon-citron hybrid, from Giovanni Batista Ferrari's *Hesperides* (1646).

in his immensely popular agriculture textbook, *Le Théâtre d'agriculture*, published in 1600. Serres (whose name is honoured in the French word for greenhouse, *serre*) recommended a special protective house with columns and a slanted roof with opening skylights and large windows, heated in winter by pans of charcoal. The citrus greenhouse became known as an orangery, though it usually contained lemon and citron trees as well. Trees were planted in wheeled boxes so they could be easily moved from place to place depending on weather conditions and the owner's wishes. Describing his own citrus trees as *magnifiques sumptuosités*, Serres acknowledged that only the rich could afford the indulgence of an orangery.

Before the greenhouse concept could really catch on, flat and transparent glass had to be available for its windows. (Before this, people used thin sheets of translucent mica to cover garden hot beds and for windows.) Although glass objects had been made for thousands of years, it wasn't until the mid-fifteenth century that Venetian glassmakers created *cristallo*, a thin, transparent glass. Yet flat clear glass panes were rare even in the seventeenth and eighteenth centuries. Glassblowers made the closest approximation by blowing a large bubble of glass and spinning it around while still soft, causing the disc to spread and flatten. After that it was cut into panes. Although such glass had dimples, concentric circles and air bubbles, at least it was transparent.

Even as the French mastered the art of grinding and polishing cast glass to produce plate glass, it was so expensive that only the rich could afford it. An orangery with a great expanse of glass was truly a luxury architectural form, a botanical novelty popular among royalty, the nobility and rich merchants. Serres dedicated his book to Henry iv, whose marriage to Marie de' Medici in 1600 brought Italian garden design to Paris, including orangeries in the Jardin des Tuileries and along the Seine. After Henry's death in 1615 Marie had her architect design gardens and an orangery for the Luxembourg Palace modelled after Florence's Boboli Gardens. Cardinal Richelieu, Marie's lifelong rival, was quick to compete, embellishing his new castle with a grand lemon-house.

No ruler was more passionate about citrus trees, particularly oranges, than Marie de' Medici's grandson, Louis xiv. The Sun King considered his gardens at Versailles an expression of his monarchy, and they consumed more water than the entire city of Paris. Citrus trees, in silver pots or giant wheeled boxes, were meticulously trained to form long, straight stems topped with rounded heads of clipped foliage, like lollipops.

 Engraving for Giovanni Battista Ferrari's *Hesperides* (1646). Glass for windows and skylights was so expensive that only the wealthy could afford an elegant citrus greenhouse, or orangery.

Shaped to the king's will, these foreign trees symbolized luxury, power and the domination of man over nature. Versailles' splendid and enormous orangery, built in 1685, was filled with citrus trees in the winter, which were moved outside in the spring and set among rose bushes, honeysuckle and jasmine to create the illusion that the trees grew directly in the soil.

Although nobody could surpass the Sun King's magnificent orangery, a kind of 'citromania' spread across northern Europe in the seventeenth and eighteenth centuries, particularly among royalty, who viewed orangeries as competitive status symbols. In Heidelberg, Germany, to celebrate his marriage to Elizabeth Stuart, Frederick v built an enormous enclosed terrace for citrus trees outside his castle, designing the roof and windows to be removed in summer so the construction would look like a giant pergola. At Kensington Palace in London an elegant greenhouse was built for Queen Anne in 1704, which she used as a winter promenade and a summer supper house. (It is now a tearoom called The Orangery.)

A merchant and botanist from Nuremberg named Johann Christoph Volkamer (1644–1720) created a delightful record of such orangeries and lemon houses connected to palaces, castles and manors. He had spent several years in Italy visiting citrus greenhouses and gardens and studying techniques of growing citrus, particularly lemons, in northern Italy's cold winters. When he returned home he built a greenhouse and became obsessed with growing lemons, oranges, citrons and limes in his grand Nuremberg garden. Wanting to show his credentials as a botanist as well as a citrus grower, Volkamer documented and classified his citrus collection and employed draughtsmen and engravers to illustrate it in 100 folio-size plates, published in 1708 as *Nürnbergische Hesperides*.

J. C. Volkamer, *Nürnbergische Hesperides* (1708), engraving. Royalty, especially Louis xiv, liked to shape citrus trees with straight stems and rounded heads, signifying man's domination over nature.

The name Hesperides came from the Greek myth of a fabulous garden boasting a tree with golden fruit. Volkamer's work echoed an earlier *Hesperides* about citrus created by a Jesuit priest named Giovanni Battista Ferrari, a horticultural advisor to the papal family and manager of Rome's fabulous Barberini Palace garden. Ferrari's book, published in 1646, was one of the first systematic studies of citrus. Although it didn't advance the *science* of citrus growing (for example, it advised burying a dead dog near tree roots to resolve disease problems), its extensive description, classification and illustrations of citrons, lemons and oranges greatly contributed to botanical knowledge. Ferrari owed much to the research and collections of his associate, a citrus-besotted scholar named Cassiano dal Pozzo, whose name was not included as author. The beautifully illustrated book featured 80 botanical plates rendered by seven artists, each showing citrus leaves

Giovanni Battista Ferrari's work *Hesperides* (1646) added greatly to the botanical knowledge of citrus. It was illustrated by engravers, with the name of each variety announced on distinctive ribboned labels, as with the Amalfi lemon here.

J. C. Volkamer, engraving from *Nürnbergische Hesperides* (1708). Volkamer modelled his great treatise on citrus after Ferrari's, while adding landscapes showing palaces, estates, manors and gardens to the botanical illustrations of whole and cut fruit.

The bizarre 'Limon Striatus Amalphitanus', probably a lemon-citron hybrid, was presented in *Hesperides* by Giovanni Battista Ferrari (1646).

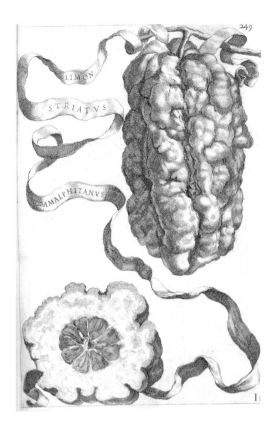

and fruits, whole and cut open, with fanciful curving ribbons announcing their names.

Half a century later, Volkamer borrowed Ferrari's style of showing whole and cut fruit with beribboned labels, but added his signature touch, filling the lower part of the plates with delightful views of gardens, palaces and landscapes in Italy and Germany. Volkamer's monograph is regarded as one of the most beautiful botanical works of the baroque period and depicts many citrus varieties no longer grown.

Lemon Houses (*Limonaie*)

In Limone, a northern Italian town on Lake Garda bordering Austria, the Dolomite mountains swoop down from the Alps and hug the lake, wedging residents into a narrow slice between water and rock. It seems an unlikely place to grow subtropical fruit. Yet in the seventeenth century it became the northernmost place in the world to grow lemons.

In fact, the lake's great volume has a moderating effect on the climate, and the mountains curve around the lake's head like a cupped hand, shielding the area from northern winds. Those factors must have convinced Carlo Bettoni and his sons, who arrived there in the mid-1600s and bought land, that farming lemons would be economically feasible – provided the trees could be protected in winter. Rather than choosing the orangery style of growing trees in moveable pots, the Bettoni family and other Lake Garda farmers built

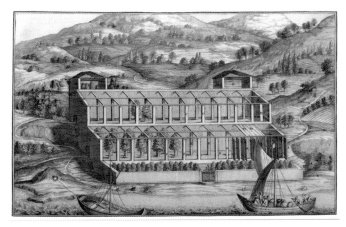

J. C. Volkamer, 'A Lemon House of Garda', from *Nürnbergische Hesperides* (1708), engraving. To learn how to grow citrus in Germany, Volkamer studied the lemon houses of Lake Garda, Italy, the northernmost place in the world to grow lemons.

Lemon picking. Every spring, the walls and roofs of the lemon houses were dismantled and stored. Pickers harvested the fruit from the terraces using special ladders or three-legged stools.

limonaie, lemon houses, up the hillsides, planting the trees in the soil and building a temporary shelter around them each autumn.

Unlike extravagant orangeries built for pleasure or ostentation, these northern Italian lemon houses had a different purpose altogether: commercial agriculture. Whereas orangeries resulted in pots of flowering or fruiting trees which could be conveniently transported to adorn villas and palaces, Lake Garda lemon houses, though very labour-intensive to construct each autumn, produced bigger, higher-quality fruit, an economic advantage for growers. And there was an eager market for these lemons. For centuries before transportation from Sicily or Southern Italy was practical, buyers from the north – Germans, Austrians, Hungarians, Poles and Russians – bought lemons from Lake Garda.

Constructing a lemon house was an arduous process. Workers carved terraces into rocky hillsides, planted lemon trees on them, dug irrigation channels on each level and built stone stairs to connect the terraces. Next, they set rows of tall stone pillars throughout the structure and laid a slanted open grid of chestnut beams atop them. They built a massive stone wall around three sides of the structure and a separate building to store roofing materials.

On a splendid morning in September 1786 Johann Wolfgang von Goethe sailed past Limone and described its 'beautiful lush terraced gardens perched on the hill slope'. Each orchard, he wrote in *Italian Journey*,

> consists of rows of square white pillars, set some distance apart and mounting the hill in steps. Stout poles are laid across these pillars to give protection during the winter to the trees which have been planted between them. Our slow progress favoured contemplation and observation of such pleasing details.[3]

Far less pleasing was the strenuous process of sealing the lemon houses from the frosts, which was done before St Catherine's Day on 25 November. Workmen carried heavy wooden planks from the storehouses to the lemon orchards and laid them pillar-to-pillar, 9 metres (30 feet) high, hammering planks to beams to form the roof. Next they tackled the open front of the building, filling in the spaces between the pillars with a wall of wooden panels, some hinged to become doors, and vertical bands of overlapping glass panes to let in some light. Dry grasses were used to seal all the gaps.

The *limonaie* used far less glass than decorative orangeries, so they were rather dark and gloomy, with only thin stripes of sunlight filtering between panels of wood. But considering the expense of glass, lemon houses were also much more economical, and still effective given that wintering citrus trees need warmth more than light. When temperatures dipped below freezing, farmers lit fires along the terraces to warm the delicate trees. Each spring the roof and front wall were dismantled and put back into storage.

Lake Garda lemons were harvested several times a year between May and October, sorted by size and quality, wrapped in tissue paper and packed in wooden boxes to be sent to various northern destinations.

Germans, who have long romanticized sunny Italy, rhapsodized about Lake Garda and its lemons, their first taste of

Centuries of isolation for Limone ended after a road tunnelling through the mountains was completed in 1931. Although the lemon houses were by then much diminished, those remaining tried to take advantage of increasing tourism by selling lemons by the side of the road.

the golden south after crossing the Alps. Goethe immortalized the area in a famous poem: '*Kennst du das Land, wo di Zitronen blühn?*' – 'Do you know the land where the lemon trees bloom?' Yet the glory days for Lake Garda lemon trees were over by the late 1800s as tree diseases and colder winters took their toll. Competition increased from southern regions, with lower production costs and improved transportation. One after another, lemon houses were abandoned. During the First World War soldiers carried away the wooden beams and planks to build shelters or use as firewood.

Today, along the northern shores of Lake Garda, you can still see tall square white stone pillars stepping up the hillsides in rows, an architectural patchwork that evokes ancient fortifications or temple ruins, as D. H. Lawrence remarked when he lived in the area in 1912. And long after the lemon trees themselves disappeared from their sojourn in the Alps, something of their legacy remains in northerners' appreciation of the taste, sight and smell of lemons, whether the Russian taste for lemon slices in tea or the German and Austrian fondness for lemon zest in pastries. The pillars, representing the tremendous labour of growing lemons at the foot of the Alps, bear witness to how much northerners loved lemons – and how much they were willing to pay for their pleasure.

4
The Lemon Cure

The summer of 1519 was a frenzy of activity on the Puerto de las Muelas dock in Seville, as sailors and dockworkers checked and stocked provisions for a fleet of five black ships. Among the workers loading rations was a short man with a limp and a Portuguese accent: Ferdinand Magellan, the captain of what was to be an extraordinary voyage to encircle the globe.

Magellan had spent lavishly on victuals for his 265-man crew, for he considered them essential not only to maintain life but to boost the crew's health and morale. So there were thousands of pounds of salted beef and pork, dried tuna, cod, sardines and anchovies. There were seven cows and three pigs, to be slaughtered at the beginning of the voyage. More than a ton of ship's biscuit, sacks of flour, beans and rice, gallons of olive oil, strings of onions and garlic. An abundance of almonds in the shell, Malaga raisins, figs, honey, sugar. Giant wheels of cheese – 'none but the best quality'. And 508 barrels of wine 'of superior vintage' from Jerez, costing more than the ship's armaments, enough to provide each man with nearly a pint a day.

Yet with all this meticulous attention to quality, Magellan failed to provide the one food that could have safeguarded the health of his crew, a food plentiful in Spain and capable of keeping for weeks without refrigeration: lemons.

Plague of the Sea

Magellan's voyage was beset with troubles. Violent electrical storms, squalls, gale-force winds, blinding snowstorms, circling sharks. Murder plots, mutiny attempts, traitors tortured and killed. Desperate hunger as food stocks rotted in the tropical heat. Yet of all these dangers, one mysterious disease, overtaking the crew in the vast Pacific Ocean, proved most deadly.

'Above all other misfortunes, this was the worst', wrote Antonio Pigafetta, a young traveller who kept a personal record of the voyage. 'The gums of some of the men swelled over their upper and lower teeth, so that they could not eat and so died of hunger.' Far from land, weakened sailors afflicted with aching limbs and swollen gums began to die, one after another. But what – aside from hunger – was the cause?

The 'plague of the sea', as sailors called it, had emerged in Europe only twenty years previously, attacking Vasco da Gama's men as they sailed around the Cape of Good Hope. An inexplicable accompaniment to the Age of Discovery, the affliction struck wildly, unevenly, with a perplexing array of symptoms. Fatigue descended upon sailors like thick fog, leaving them lethargic and morose, scarcely able to rise from their hammocks. Limbs stiffened, gums swelled and bled, victims struggled for breath. Old wounds tore open, black bruises appeared, excruciating pain surged through joints, muscles and bones. In the attack's last stages, some became unbearably sensitive: merely the *sound* of a gunshot could kill them.

'Death's dire ravage', as one poet called it, killed nearly two-thirds of Vasco da Gama's crew – and accompanied nearly every long sea expedition for the next 300 years. In two major outbreaks on Magellan's voyage, nearly half the 265-man crew perished. Those sailors who yet had strength lifted each corpse, swathed in old sailcloth, onto a plank and tied cannonballs to its feet. After a brief prayer, they lowered the plank and let the body sink beneath the waves.

A few decades after Magellan's crew succumbed to its ravages, scurvy, or scorbutus, was given its name, derived from old Icelandic *skyrbjúgur*, meaning 'cut (or ulcerated) swellings'. By the late sixteenth century Sir Richard Hawkins, a British admiral, estimated that 10,000 sailors had been 'consumed with this disease' in his twenty years in the Royal Navy. More than two million sailors died of scurvy – more than died from storms, shipwrecks, combat and all other diseases combined.[1]

Lemons could have saved countless lives, but it took a long time to figure that out. In the meantime, confusion reigned. Sometimes scurvy's symptoms were attributed to other maladies – leprosy, asthma or madness. Sometimes scurvy's effects were confused with its causes, as when fatigued sailors were told to exercise more – even dance on the dock every day – to resist the disease. 'For if you once fall to laziness and sloth, then the scarby is ready to catch you by the bones and will shake out every tooth in your head', warned the secretary of one sixteenth-century expedition.[2]

Others blamed causes beyond the victims' control. Perhaps the illness resulted from 'vapours' of the sea air, some said, wisely observing that scurvy appeared only after men had been confined to the ship for long periods. Physicians, less wisely, identified scurvy as a disease of the spleen, or attributed it to an acid–alkaline imbalance.

The first symptom of scurvy was severe fatigue, as depicted in this lithograph of 1842. Some early observers, believing that 'laziness and sloth' brought on the later symptoms, advised sailors to exercise and dance on the deck to resist the disease.

What about diet? Some blamed the high consumption of salted meat or the deterioration of long-stored food, 'the corruption of the victuals'. Yet in the sixteenth and seventeenth centuries no one ever suggested the diet could be lacking in nutrients, for the idea of dietary deficiency was still hundreds of years in the future.

A Great and Unknown Virtue

'Anti-scurvy acid', or ascorbic acid, otherwise known as vitamin C, is essential to produce collagen, the protein in connective tissue that surrounds bodily structures and holds them together. Only a few species do not produce their own ascorbic acid, among them humans, monkeys, fruit-eating bats and guinea pigs. Those species depend entirely on dietary sources to prevent scurvy.

Vitamin C dependence is not usually a perceptible problem for people unless they go for twelve weeks or more without fresh fruits or vegetables – such as in a long expedition. Then signs of unstable collagen production may appear – bleeding and swollen gums, loose teeth, stiff limbs, spots on the legs. If no vitamin C is taken, the small blood vessels weaken, tissues break down, and eventually the person will die.

Because guinea pigs are also among the few vitamin C-dependent mammals, it was serendipitous that two Norwegian scientists chose them, rather than rats, as lab animals in 1907 when trying to induce beriberi (a disease caused by lack of vitamin B1) using a diet deficient in fruits and vegetables. The scientists were startled to see the guinea pigs develop clear symptoms of scurvy instead. The experiment led to the discovery of ascorbic acid and, at last, an understanding of the cause of scurvy.

But long before people understood scurvy's cause, many believed they knew its cure. Time and again, mariners suffering from scurvy gravitated to lemon and sour orange trees as if by instinct. A scurvy-savaged crew landing on the coast of West Africa in 1582 tore into the lemons that grew there. 'God be praised', wrote the expedition's secretary. 'We see some of them amend their mouths, scouring them with the juice of lemons.' In 1593, when Hawkins's crew was afflicted with scurvy after four months at sea, they landed in southern Brazil, where the men traded cloth for 'sower oranges and lemmons', their spirits brightening simply upon seeing the fruit. In 1614 an expedition for the Dutch East India

Company stopped at Sierra Leone, 'since our crew was fast beginning to contract scurvy', and obtained 28,000 lemons. For, as Hawkins had said, citrus had a 'great and unknown virtue . . . to be a certain remedy for this infirmity'.[3]

These and many other examples seemed a most persuasive argument for a lemon cure. So why did it take the British Royal Navy so long to recognize it? In *The History of Scurvy and Vitamin C*, Kenneth Carpenter explains how the case for citrus was undermined by various factors. One particularly contrary aspect was that landing places with citrus trees could also harbour dangerous infections, fevers, malaria and dysentery. Unlike scurvy, these fevers and diseases attacked with frightening speed and were often fatal, especially to scurvy-weakened sailors.

Many observers, such as Sir James Lancaster, who led the first expedition for the British East India Company in 1601, scarcely knew what to do. On the one hand, Lancaster had unintentionally demonstrated the lemon's power. After he gave lemon juice to the men on his ship, he noted how much healthier they were than the men of the expedition's other three ships; later in the voyage, noting early signs of scurvy, he took his crew ashore at Madagascar to consume restorative lemons, 'which they did devour immoderately', and proclaimed the fruit 'the best remedy against the scurvy'. On the other hand, when sailors died of fever infections at Madagascar, Lancaster blamed the deaths on their consumption of plantains and lemons. The innocent lemon must have seemed a treacherous fruit to him: dealing health to some, death to others.

Other aspects were bewildering too. Although fresh lemons seemed almost a miracle cure, nearly every time someone tried to use preserved or concentrated lemon juice, then called 'lemon water', the results were far from convincing.

They had no way of knowing that ascorbic acid – that invisible and unknown therapeutic element in the lemons – is lost over time or with processing. The preserved juice simply didn't work, throwing the whole lemon-cure theory into doubt.[4]

In the meantime plenty of other candidates competed in the quest to cure scurvy. Oil of vitriol, or sulphuric acid, was touted as a remedy for more than a hundred years – without a shred of evidence on its behalf. Vinegar, cream of tartar, alcoholic cider and malted barley – to name but a few – were also considered credible cures. Such substances were dispensed indiscriminately and often simultaneously to the crews – making it impossible to know which one might be responsible for health or sickness. Captain Cook, for example, achieved extraordinary success in eliminating scurvy on his ships, apparently by including sauerkraut in the rations. But he had applied such a barrage of scurvy treatments, including ventilating the crew's quarters and dispensing not only sauerkraut but also malt, portable (dehydrated) soup, concentrated lemon juice, vinegar, oil of vitriol and so on, that no one could figure out which treatment was responsible for the remarkable result. There was still no reliable cure.

The Voyage to Lemon Grog

In 1740 Sir George Anson set off on Britain's first circumnavigation of the world with 2,000 men. When he returned, four years later, 1,400 men were dead, nearly all from scurvy. The remaining crew members were so weak that they had to abandon their ships.

The official account of the disastrous voyage, with its vivid and grim details, horrified the British public, pressuring naval authorities to find a cure. James Lind, a Royal Navy surgeon, decided to investigate which of the many suggested treatments had any real effect by conducting a methodical study that has been called the first controlled trial in clinical science. He isolated twelve scurvy victims and gave each of six pairs the same diet, along with a daily dose of one of the popular scurvy remedies: cider; oil of vitriol; vinegar; a paste of garlic, mustard, myrrh and balsam of Peru; seawater; or oranges and lemons.

'The most sudden and visible good effects were perceived from the use of the oranges and lemons', Lind wrote in his publication *A Treatise of the Scurvy* (1753), dedicated to Sir George Anson. All other treatments were deemed worthless.

Now a citrus solution seemed certain, but once again a big obstacle remained. Lind proposed that the citrus treatment be given *not* with fresh fruit, which could go mouldy during a long voyage, but rather with lemon juice preserved by evaporation into a thick syrup or 'rob'. Such a concoction would be effective for years, he claimed. The problem was, it wasn't true. Modern analysis of Lind's recipe shows that only one-seventh of the original vitamin C remains after just one month. In three months, when it was to be used as treatment, it would have been all but worthless.

In any case, the Royal Navy did not pursue Lind's recommendations until 1795, when Gilbert Blane, a physician who had observed devastating outbreaks of scurvy at sea, was appointed to the board in charge of ordering medical supplies. Crediting Lind's research, Blane recommended issuing lemon juice to the crews – both to cure and to prevent scurvy.

The British Navy implemented Blane's order the same year, and almost immediately conquered a persistent enemy. Fortunately, there was no attempt to use Lind's recipe for evaporated 'rob'. Over the next nineteen years 1.6 million gallons of lemon juice was issued, according to British naval

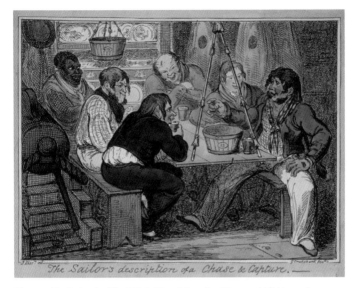

George Cruikshank, *The Sailor's Description of a Chase and Capture*, 1822, etching. A tub of grog is on the table, while another hangs from the roof.

records, most coming through Malta. The juice was stored in casks under a layer of olive oil, which preserved most of its ascorbic acid. Fresh lemons were preserved by pickling or salting before being wrapped in paper, so they could be squeezed as needed. After the ship had been at sea for five or six weeks, every sailor was to receive a daily dose of lemon juice.

For a time in the mid-nineteenth century the Admiralty switched to limes rather than lemons, so they could use fruit grown in the British West Indies. Lime juice, however, was found to be far less effective and scurvy flared up again. Still, British sailors were dubbed 'Limeys', a term still used.

Whether lemon or lime, sailors took their ration of sour juice willingly, since it was combined with a more popular ration: rum. Since the 1770s the rum-and-water ration named 'grog' had been a feature of British sailors' lives. It was named for its inventor, Admiral Edward Vernon, who was nicknamed 'Old Grog' for his waterproof cloak of grogram, a coarse, loosely woven fabric. Vernon insisted on watering the sailors' rum rations, mixing one pint of rum with two of water. After 1795 the name 'grog' was applied to the new mixture, which now included lemon juice.

The Legacy of the Lemon Cure

The lemon has never played a more vital role in history. As sailors drank their grog, the curse of scurvy, which had appeared on Vasco da Gama's voyage 300 years before, virtually disappeared. Some even claim that the superior health enjoyed by Admiral Nelson's crew helped the British defeat Napoleon at Trafalgar in 1805, ensuring Britain's supremacy as a naval power for the next century.

Even more certainly, the Royal Navy's new rations created a thriving market for Mediterranean lemons from Spain, Sicily and Italy. One of the more interesting effects of that demand occurred along the Amalfi and Sorrentine coasts of Southern Italy, where lemons had been grown intensively for hundreds of years, harvested when still green and kept cool in caves so they could be available in every season.

With the dramatic surge in overseas sales in the 1800s, Amalfi lemon growers on a slender curve of arable land along the Tyrrhenian Sea searched for more land. There was nowhere to go but up. Breaking rock with picks and explosives, they built containment walls and filled narrow terraces with soil carried from chestnut forests above. Small, carefully tended lemon gardens rose on the hillsides like layers on a wedding cake with 30 or 40 tiers. Pickers harvested lemons into chestnut baskets; women wearing cotton gloves sorted them, wrapped them in tissue and packed them into flexible poplar boxes bound by chestnut hoops, both protecting the fruit and allowing it to ripen during shipping.

After the First World War high-volume sales for Italian lemons dwindled as California and other larger commercial suppliers competed for the overseas market and the British Navy's demand for lemons fell as commercially produced vitamin C became available in the late 1930s. In this coastline region of Italy, however, traditional growing methods continued, producing the region's high-quality lemons, today considered some of the finest in the world.

Another legacy of the lemon's triumph against scurvy can be seen in Britain's appreciation for the fruit. While Americans use the word 'lemon' with negative connotations, you will not find a similarly disparaging association in British usage. For there, for more than a century, the lemon saved lives.

5
Lemonade

Whether hot or cold, lemonade held a strong reputation as a healthy drink even before it was known to cure scurvy. In his twelfth-century treatise the Egyptian physician Ibn Jumay had written that lemonade 'quenches one's thirst and revives one's strength' and could treat everything from throat inflammations and indigestion to hangovers.

In sixteenth-century Britain, with lemons still very costly, a physician might prescribe health-restoring lemonade or 'water imperial', an infusion of pearl barley and water with cream of tartar, sugar and lemon juice. Such recommendations appeared in the 'invalid cookery' sections of British cookbooks into the nineteenth and twentieth centuries. Isabella Beeton's *Book of Household Management* (1861), for example, called lemonade helpful for both 'bilious and sanguine temperaments', offering recipes for basic 'lemonade for invalids' and 'nourishing lemonade' including eggs and sherry.

Lemonade – especially when it was ice-cold – was also consumed for pure pleasure in warm climates where both lemons and sugar were plentiful. The two crops share the same birthplace and route to the Mediterranean, traceable through the Sanskrit, Persian and Arabic roots of their names. In India a cooling drink called *nimbu paani*, which combines freshly

Sunkist Lemons brochure, 1939.

squeezed lemons, sugar, salt and sometimes pepper or other spices, is considered especially refreshing. Persian and Arabic *sharbat* and Sicilian granita are basically frozen forms of lemonade. Bottled lemon juice, generously sweetened with sugar, was very popular in medieval Egypt and enjoyed a robust export trade.[1]

The delightful beverage did not catch on as quickly in northern Europe, however, since imported lemons were too expensive for the populace to enjoy. There was also the problem of sweetener. Honey, the most common sweetener in medieval Europe, was in short supply after beehives were destroyed or abandoned during the religious wars of the late Middle Ages. And sugar, grown in the West Indies and Brazil, was prohibitively expensive until the early 1600s. Lemonade in northern Europe before that time remained either a necessary expense for the ill or a privilege for the very rich.

A Drink for the People

For common folk, there was water. In Paris itinerant water vendors learned to add a few drops of vinegar to the water to make it more refreshing and disguise any off-flavours. But around 1630 all that changed. The expansion of sugar plantations in the West Indies – along with the malevolent practice of slave labour – led to a collapse in the price of sugar. Suddenly *limonade*, made with lemons, water and sugar, became affordable. Ordinary people embraced it in a great gush of popularity. Sales of vinegar declined as water vendors became *limonadiers* or lemonade-men, dispensing the fresh sweet-tart beverage from metal tanks carried on their backs.

French cookbooks of the mid-1600s offered scores of lemonade recipes, scented and flavoured with exotic spices and flowers: ambergris, musk, cinnamon, rosewater, jasmine, orange blossoms, carnations. 'Lemonade is prepared in different ways according to the different ingredients used', wrote François Pierre de La Varenne in *Le Cuisinier françois* ('The French Cook', 1651). For jasmine or orange blossom lemonade, he recommended infusing a couple of pints of water with two handfuls of flowers for eight to ten hours before combining with lemon juice and sugar. Nicolas de Bonnefons, valet to Louis XIII, wrote a whole chapter on 'Lemonades' in his book *Les Délices de la campagne* ('The Pleasures of the Countryside', 1662). In a typical recipe coriander seed and cinnamon are infused in a mixture of lemon peel, juice and powdered sugar, strained through linen and bottled. 'If you like you may add musk and ambergris to give it a more pleasant taste', he wrote.

In 1676 the French government granted *limonadiers* a patent for the exclusive right to sell 'all kinds of ambered and scented lemonade', as well as hot coffee, tea and chocolate,

Charles Philibon, *Le Garçon limonadier*, 1827–9, hand-coloured lithograph. The *limonadiers* began as street vendors but soon began to sell their beverages in elegant cafes.

wines, sugar plums, brandied fruits, syrups and jellies. Merchants in the newly formed guild, which had merged with the distillers, were called *limonadiers* in the seventeenth and eighteenth centuries, although they sold many beverages besides lemonade.

Francesco Procopio dei Coltelli, a Sicilian-born *limonadier* in his mid-twenties, was selling lemonade, hot coffee and other treats from three stalls in Paris during the annual late

Eduoard Manet, *The Lemon*, 1880, oil on canvas.

winter fair when he bought his guild membership. He was to become the most famous *limonadier* of all after he opened Café Procope on the rue des Fossés-Saint-Germain-des-Prés in 1686.

At the time, Paris beverage houses were dark cramped places, nothing like London's spacious coffee houses where people gathered for coffee and news. But Procopio decorated his cafe with large expensive mirrors, crystal chandeliers, marble tables and beautiful glass bottles filled with jewel-coloured liquids. Boys in Turkish-style costumes served lemon-ade, coffee and hot chocolate in silver or porcelain drinking bowls. After a company of actors brought together by Molière opened a theatre across the street, the success of Café Procope was ensured. Actors, poets, artists, writers, businessmen and politicians hobnobbed there from morning till night – and Parisian cafe society was born.

America's Innocent Refreshment

The American painter Raphaelle Peale, in the tradition of seventeenth-century Dutch still-life artists, paid homage to a well-matched duo in his *Lemons and Sugar* (1822), showing a decorated porcelain sugar bowl next to a basket of golden lemons. The lemons in Peale's painting, like those in Dutch art centuries before, represented something rare and valuable – and most likely imported. Until nearly the end of the nineteenth century, American lemonade was often made with foreign lemons.

Citrus is not native to the Americas and had been unknown until Columbus brought lemon, orange and citron seeds from the Canary Islands to Haiti on his second voyage, in 1493. The Caribbean climate was so favourable that orchards swelled

When the American artist Raphaelle Peale painted *Lemons and Sugar* in 1822, the lemons were most likely imported from Sicily. Americans relied on imported lemons until the early 1900s.

into citrus forests within a few generations. The Portuguese brought lemons to Brazil by 1540, and in 1788 the captain of the First Fleet of British colonists carried lemon trees from Rio de Janeiro to Australia. Spanish explorers and colonists introduced citrus to Florida by the mid-1500s, but commercial cultivation in Florida and California did not begin until the mid-1800s, and Florida's lemon industry collapsed in the mid-1890s after a disastrous freeze.

Before the early 1900s, most lemons from California were a disappointment. Eastern US fruit merchants complained about the fruit's poor condition. The quality of most California-grown lemons was so low that expensive lemons imported from the Mediterranean competed with them even in Los Angeles and San Francisco markets.[2] The American use of the word 'lemon' to mean something that fails to live up to standards may have developed around this time because it was so hard to find a satisfactory American-grown lemon.

Besides investing in expensive lemons, American lemonade makers also had to pay high prices and tariffs for imported sugar. Until domestic production of beet sugar began in the 1880s, it was an extravagant venture to make lemonade or other sugar-sweetened lemon desserts.

One group decided it was worth the cost: the Shakers, a religious sect founded in Britain that had established American communities in the early nineteenth century. Although the Shakers were decidedly frugal and nearly self-sufficient, they made an exception for lemons, considering them such a necessity that they were the first food purchased for their colony in North Union, Ohio. They threw away little of this precious fruit, macerating both rinds and pulp for lemon pie filling, and pouring boiling water over lemon rinds to add to lemonade. An 1881 issue of the *Shakers' Manifesto* described lemonade as 'one of the healthiest and most refreshing of all

Citrus fruit label. Fancy glass pitchers for serving lemonade to guests became popular in the USA in the late 1800s, after the Temperance movement adopted the beverage.

drinks'. American medical practitioners evidently agreed, prescribing lemonade to promote a cheerful disposition.

Lemonade also had another quality the Shakers valued: it was, or at least could be, non-alcoholic. The practice of spiking lemonade with alcohol is nearly as old as the beverage itself; in 1299 the Mongols were enjoying sweetened lemon juice preserved with alcohol, and British sailors in 1795 consumed more rum than lemon juice in their lemonade grog. Bartenders in America followed suit, serving up lemonades with wine and spirits.

But as the American Temperance movement gathered steam in the mid-1800s, adherents promoted non-alcoholic beverages to substitute for the evils of alcohol and even coffee. The already popular lemonade, along with ginger beer, spruce beer and soda pop, now became a favoured 'Temperance drink', wholesome and innocent. In the 1870s

First Lady Lucy Webb Hayes, wife of nineteenth president Rutherford B. Hayes, banned nearly all alcohol in the White House and was dubbed 'Lemonade Lucy', giving the drink further recognition.

Early American recipes for lemonade, derived from British recipes, sometimes sounded more like sherbet and at other times included milk or egg. Some used lemon syrups while others were basic mixtures of water, sugar, lemon juice and rind.

Effervescent or carbonated waters had been manufactured since the eighteenth century, when they were thought to have medicinal value. Sweetened soda waters soon followed, and lemonade, already popular, was one of the first. More than a million effervescent beverages, including soda water, ginger ale and lemonade, were sold at the Great Exhibition of 1851 in London. In America carbonated lemonade and other soda waters were often sold at 'soda fountains', fashionable gathering places promoted by Temperance advocates as alternatives to saloons. By 1895 approximately 50,000 soda parlours were dispensing such fizzy drinks (as well as ice cream) across the usa.

But it was the non-carbonated version of lemonade that stuck in America. Its popularity soared with the new ease of making the beverage at home and its pleasurable associations. Lemon squeezers had been hinged two-handled affairs that were fairly ineffective, but the Sears Roebuck Catalogue of 1897 introduced an improved glass lemon squeezer with a ribbed dome and rim to catch the juice. Specially designed glass pitchers were fashionable for serving lemonade on the front porch. At summertime picnics and parties, refreshing lemonade became the drink of choice.

Soda fountains and luncheonettes, which profited greatly from Prohibition's enactment in 1920, also found it easier to

The lemonade stand has become an American fixture during the summer months.

offer fresh lemonade once the California Fruit Growers Exchange began manufacturing and selling electric citrus juicers in 1922. By 1932 about 66,000 Sunkist juice extractors were in operation.

Fairs, circuses, carnivals, seaside boardwalks – lemonade became linked with these summertime entertainments as firmly as ice cream and hot dogs. Pink lemonade was particularly associated with circuses, and a curious legend developed about its origin. Supposedly, a circus vendor named Henry Allott invented this drink in the 1870s after he accidentally dropped some red cinnamon candies in a batch of lemonade. The story sounds apocryphal since cookbooks of the period often suggested flavouring lemonade with pink or red fruit such as watermelon, raspberries, strawberries and cherries – and flavoured varieties were nothing new. Yet the *Washington*

Post's obituary for Allott in 1912 accepted legend as fact, describing 'pink lemonade in glasses set in trays, with a straw in each and a piece of lemon floating on top', adding, '25 years ago every boy and man . . . would have said that if pink lemonade went the circus must fall with it'.

The Italian Connection

Meanwhile, immigrants from Sicily were flooding into New Orleans, bringing with them a passion for lemons and a type of frozen lemonade. Steamships from Palermo arriving at the port of New Orleans from 1880 onward were nicknamed 'lemon boats' since they carried cargoes of lemons as well as hundreds of immigrants who had worked in Sicily as citrus farmers or pedlars. Many disembarked clutching containers of lemons. So many Sicilians arrived that the French Quarter was dubbed 'Little Sicily' and 'Little Palermo'. Most were peasants fleeing the poverty of their homeland, and they worked alongside African Americans as labourers on the docks or in the *zuccarata*, the annual sugar cane harvest on plantations along the Mississippi River. Others used their connections in Sicily to become importers and distributors of fruit, particularly citrus. Still others sold a thirst-quenching iced and sugared lemon confection much like granita at lemonade stands on the streets of the city.

Local sugar, fresh lemons and the stifling heat of New Orleans made iced lemonade or granita-like confections a success, especially with the availability of manufactured ice. Mark Twain described an ice factory along the Mississippi which from 1883 produced 30 tons of ice a day, and he visited a New Orleans factory that sold blocks of ice for as little as $6 or $7 a ton.

Vendors of icy lemonade or 'Italian ice' in the northern states also operated pushcarts or stands, both on city streets and in recreation areas like the Jersey Shore. One example of a stand that is both traditional and contemporary is Mario's Italian Lemonade on Taylor Street in Chicago's Little Italy, where a horse and buggy delivered ice in 100-lb (45-kg) blocks as late as the early 1960s. Like many such stands, Mario's is open only in the summer months, when residents seek relief from the sweltering heat. Countless Chicagoans define summer by Mario's lemonade stand's opening and closing dates, and on any hot, humid day or evening from the first day of May to mid-September, dozens of people line up for a paper cup filled with one of the twenty flavours of icy lemonade.

In 1962, when Italian immigrant Mario DiPaolo and his wife Dorothy set up the stand next to their general store, lemonade sold for two cents or a nickel and was served in

Immigrants from Sicily and Italy brought a passion for lemons and lemonade with them to America.

The *coolingest cooler of all* - **Sunkist Lemonade**

THERE YOU ARE. Stretched out in the shade. A tall, frosty glass of fresh Sunkist lemonade in your hand. You sip it, enjoy its tangy, fresh fragrance. You take a long, cold swallow. And suddenly...*coolness.* Deep. All through you.

There's your proof. Lemonade refreshes more thoroughly than any other summer drink. The reason is simple. Lemon juice replaces vitamin C and other energy-giving vitamins that warm weather takes away.

For true lemon flavor and long-lasting refreshment, drink Sunkist lemonade. Lots of it. Sunkist Lemons are the pick of the crop!

TRY FRESH LEMON WITH ICED TEA! Lemon brings out the flavor and delicate aroma of the tea, adds a subtle, delicious tang, makes it even more cooling and refreshing. Iced tea... wedges of lemon... wonderful for sparking up summer meals! Remember lemons—today.

NOW—Sunkist FROZEN LEMONADE! When you're extra busy, here's delicious lemonade we make for you. A fine, new Sunkist product now coming on the market. Just add water and ice. *Easy. Healthful. Refreshing!* Look for it! **FRESH OR FROZEN, IT'S BEST WHEN IT'S Sunkist!**

Sunkist Lemons FROM CALIFORNIA

In the USA, lemonade became a symbol of summer relaxation, as portrayed in this advertisement of 1951, when frozen lemonade had just been developed for the mass market.

pleated paper squeeze cups, without a spoon. Originally the lemons were cut and squeezed by hand and the lemonade achieved its icy texture in a wooden hand-cranked machine, said the founders' son, also named Mario DiPaolo. Lemons are still sliced in half by hand and squeezed, one by one, on a professional juicer that extracts the whole pulp, including the seeds.

Unlike many sellers of Italian iced lemonade, Mario's Italian Lemonade does not use any artificial flavourings or syrups. The lemonade formula is simply sugar, lemons and water; other flavours, such as watermelon, are made by adding fresh fruit to the base. And, echoing the Shakers, Mario's uses every part of the lemon, with nothing going to waste. 'We're still using lemons, whole lemons, not just the juice', DiPaolo says. 'To make good lemonade you need all of the lemon – including the pulp, the rind, the seeds.'

Not everyone has been so principled about the ingredients in lemonade. A grocer's notes from the early 1880s reveal that many vendors used tartaric acid to imitate lemon flavour, merely floating lemon slices on the surface to give the impression of authenticity. And a Sunkist booklet of 1911 warned: 'When ordering lemonade, insist that fresh lemons only are used. Injurious acids are frequently substituted.'

These days there are powdered lemonade mixes that supply a tart flavour by means of citric acid and include artificial colour. Frozen lemonade concentrate was introduced in the 1950s, advertised by Sunkist as 'the coolingest cooler of them all'. Bottled lemonade is widely available as well.

Though soda drinks are far and away the most favoured of sweet beverages, Americans still hold a special affection for lemonade – the drink of summer and happy carefree times.

6

To and From the Golden State

In the summer of 1893 tens of thousands of visitors flocked to see one beautiful little California citrus orchard: 30 orange trees, twenty lemon trees. They admired the full leafy green trees 'gemmed with much ripened fruit' and inhaled the exquisite scent of abundant citrus blossoms.

These sightseers were not actually in California but rather at the World's Columbian Exposition in Chicago, where California was showing off its prize crop to the world. There were thousands of fresh oranges and lemons wired into enormous sculptures – a tower topped by an eagle, a gigantic globe, a life-size replica of the Liberty Bell. But this living orchard, with every tree bearing fruit and blossoms, topped everything.

The orchard's journey to the Chicago World's Fair had been carefully planned and orchestrated. Transporting live subtropical plants on such a scale had never succeeded before in the USA. A year or two before the fair, the trees were dug up and transplanted into large boxes to give them time to adjust to the shock. After reaching Chicago via the Southern Pacific railroad, they were replanted. Tended like royalty, the trees flourished, growing and bearing fruit until the end of the fair.

'This surprising display awakened lively interest in myriads of visitors', noted the report from the California World's Fair Commission, 'especially among those who, living all their lives under sterner skies, had never before had the privilege of enjoying such a sight or even seeing a single bearing orange or lemon tree'.

Lemon Lands

It was also in the summer of 1893 that a young man named Charles Collins Teague rode a train from Kansas to Southern California, a move that was to transform the American lemon industry. Teague's great-uncle, a rich oil man with a passion for citrus, had recently joined up with pioneer citrus grower Nathan Blanchard to plant 400 acres of lemon trees in Santa Paula, California. They called their ranch Limoneira, a name said to mean 'lemon lands' in Portuguese.

With Nathan Blanchard's guidance, Teague learned all he could about growing lemons, revealing a natural talent for it. Under his management, a 40-acre plot purchased with his great-uncle, the Teague Forty, attained agricultural renown as one of the world's most productive lemon orchards. Teague learned which rootstocks to select, when to pick, and how to deal with problems of pests, diseases and damage from sun, wind or frost. He refined irrigation methods, introduced the 'Teague Method' of storing winter lemons for the summer market and solved deterioration problems with controlled temperature and humidity, ventilated storage and shipping. From Nathan Blanchard he learned to treat each lemon as delicately as an egg.

These advances had a great impact on the fledgling industry. Before the early 1900s, as we have seen, many buyers rejected California lemons, even though imported fruit might cost five times as much. Eastern fruit merchants complained that California lemons were carelessly packed and weren't fresh when they arrived. 'Those who used them profaned over their efforts to extract any juice from them', wrote lemon pioneer G. W. Garcelon in 1891.[1] California lemons had 'a grievous competitor in the imported Sicily fruit and the popular favoritism for it', wrote the author of an agricultural manual in 1899.[2]

Limoneira's fruit proved an exception. Blanchard and Teague – the astute pioneer and the innovative manager – had vastly improved the growing, grading, packing and storing methods, and insisted on ventilated railroad cars for shipment. A merchant in Chicago, upon receiving a shipment of Limoneira's lemons, declared: 'I do not think that any better lemons grow on earth.'

Lemon crate label. Prior to 1848, California was part of Mexico, and California's first citrus was grown at Spanish missions, so images reflecting the Spanish / Mexican heritage have been associated with California fruit-packing companies since the beginning of the industry.

In 1905, lemon pickers at Limoneira Ranch filled wooden boxes of fruit, which were hauled by horse and cart.

Throughout California, lemon growers regarded Limoneira Ranch as a model of fruit growing and handling. 'I might say that it is getting to be a sort of lemon Jerusalem', Teague wrote in 1902, 'toward which pilgrimages are being made from all over the lemon country.'[3] With Teague as manager and president, Limoneira Ranch would become the world's largest lemon producer, a veritable lemon empire.

Sunkist Sells

Romanticized descriptions of Southern California's 'Paradise on Earth' lured droves of settlers and would-be citrus growers from the eastern states. One of these, Eliza Tibbets, ordered two Brazilian navel orange trees from the US Department of Agriculture in 1873 and thus launched the California orange industry. Transcontinental railways brought citrus to fairs and exhibits, opening up eastern markets. Before long, citrus orchards stretched across Southern California.

The coastal areas were ideal for growing lemons. Frost-sensitive lemons thrive in the mild climate and, unlike oranges, lemons don't need hot days to develop sugar. The Mediterranean climate encourages trees to blossom and bear fruit all year long so crops can be harvested four or five times a year. By 1900 the Santa Barbara area was described as 'the most suitable location possible for the production of the lemon'. Orchards carpeted the foothills, perfuming the coastline with the scent of lemon blossoms.

In the mid-1880s citrus growers formed cooperative organizations and created catchy brand names to distinguish their products. They hired lithographers in San Francisco and Los Angeles to design colourful paper labels for their wooden citrus crates to capture the attention of eastern buyers. The

Lemon crate label. In 1899 a writer described the Carpinteria Valley, near Santa Barbara: 'besides possessing the most perfect climate in the known world [it is] . . . about the most suitable location possible for the production of the lemon.'

From the 1880s to the 1950s, lithographed labels which were pasted on wooden citrus crates used appealing images and catchy brand names to attract buyers. The California Fruit Growers Exchange used the Red Ball logo for its second-best fruit.

attractive labels were not only effective marketing tools but also indicators of the fruit's grade. The most cosmetically pleasing citrus received a top grade designation such as the Sunkist, while lower-grade fruit was indicated with a designation such as the Red Ball logo. Before the era of citrus labels ended in the 1950s with the advent of preprinted cardboard cartons, more than 8,000 distinct labels had been designed and used.

The biggest advance in citrus selling began in 1893, when a group of prominent citrus growers formed the Southern California Fruit Exchange to market and distribute fruit. Renamed the California Fruit Growers Exchange in 1905 and Sunkist Growers in 1952, it was to become the largest marketing cooperative of produce in the world. It was also the first in the USA to advertise a perishable food product. Initially,

Lemon crate label. The California Fruit Growers Exchange, a cooperative of citrus growers, adopted the Sunkist brand name in 1908, and used the Sunkist logo for its highest quality fruit.

growers were reluctant to spend much on advertising, but after the Southern Pacific Railroad offered matching funds for a five-month test promotion in the state of Iowa, they could hardly refuse. Special citrus trains labelled with banners rolled into Iowa in 1908, and the state was inundated with colour newspaper ads, citrus displays, posters and poetry contests. Shops offered special sales of oranges and lemons wrapped in tissues stamped with the memorable name 'Sunkist'. As sales of citrus skyrocketed, both growers and the railroad saw profits rolling in. The next year they expanded the campaign's geographical reach as well as its budget.

With the Iowa campaign's slogan, 'Oranges for Health, California for Wealth', Sunkist pioneered the advertising of food through touting its health benefits. Some claims were of dubious scientific value. A booklet published around 1910 promoted Sunkist lemon juice as a powerful germicide, 'rich

This Sunkist booklet of *c.* 1910 offered health claims along with recipes for pies and suggestions for cosmetic uses. 'The juice of a Sunkist lemon is a powerful germicide, completely destroying those minute organisms which cause and prolong nearly all diseases', the text read.

in organic salts, which is nature's medicine', capable of treating everything from pulmonary diseases to bee stings and acne. Warm lemonade was said to sweeten the stomach, regulate the liver and reduce 'the overabundance of flesh'.

C. C. Teague of Limoneira, who had been involved in the cooperative from the early years, was elected president of the Exchange in 1920 and held the position until his death 30 years later. He was a strong advocate for Sunkist's nationwide advertising and considered its large budget a good investment. The 'Drink an Orange' campaign of 1916 had changed the way American families consumed oranges, he noted, causing a big leap in sales.

Lemon growers also saw sales increase as Sunkist advertisements promoted the fruit not only for lemonade and cooking but also for mouthwash, cosmetics, household cleaning and, above all, health. In 1918 Sunkist became the first national advertiser in the USA to mention vitamins – known then as 'vitamines' – essential substances in food that could protect against scurvy, beriberi, pellagra and rickets, according to a Polish biochemist named Casimir Funk. Lemon juice 'furnishes the vitamines . . . necessary for *balance* in the diet', said an advert published in the *Ladies Home Journal*. 'The lemon is too important as a *dietary aid* to be omitted from your meals.'

In the 1930s, even as the Depression deepened, lemon growers were thriving, selling their crop at remarkably high prices. Besides Limoneira, one of the most successful operations was the Johnston Fruit Company, incorporated in 1897. J. Harleigh Johnston, who had spent a year in Italy learning about cultivating lemons, packed fruit for growers throughout Santa Barbara County. Located near the Southern Pacific railroad line and Santa Barbara's main wharf, the Johnston Fruit Company packing houses shipped boxes of lemons around the world by rail or steamer.

'No group of farmers or growers anywhere have come through the Depression in as good shape as the lemon growers of California', boasted Teague in a radio broadcast on citrus marketing in 1938. Their success, he said, was 'because advertised Sunkist fruit commands a big price premium in markets everywhere'.[4] Yet Teague's next radio broadcast emphasized the need to increase demand. Noting that many

This Sunkist advert of 1918 promoted lemons for both culinary and health purposes.

In this booklet dating from 1935 Sunkist suggested making lemon shampoos, hair rinses, skin cleansers and creams. Lemon juice was recommended for soothing baths, removing freckles and blemishes and weight loss.

uses for lemon – flavouring, decoration, hair rinse, cosmetics – had been popularized by Sunkist advertising, he announced a new promotion: 'simply the drinking of lemon juice, water and bicarbonate of soda each morning or evening as a mild laxative', requiring the use of one lemon a day. 'If we can get one person in a hundred to use a lemon a day, we will have increased the national consumption by 20 per cent!' Teague said, concluding with an exhortation: 'We need the increased demand. We are going after it for all we are worth.'[5]

Teague believed in the power of lemons, in the most personal sense. He had broken his hip in a childhood accident and as an adult suffered from painful and debilitating arthritis. Doctors locally and at the Johns Hopkins Hospital in Baltimore, Maryland, were no help, but he discovered the best remedy in Limoneira's orchard: lemons. At first he drank the juice of two or three lemons with water every day; later, he increased this to two lemons with each meal and two before bed, making a total of eight lemons a day. Lemon juice, he claimed, not only eased his arthritis but also cured another long-term problem: indigestion.[6]

An extreme version of Teague's lemon regime, a 'detoxifying' lemonade fast, was created in the 1940s by Stanley Burroughs, an advocate of alternative health treatments. He believed that drinking water with fresh lemon juice, maple syrup and a little cayenne – and eating nothing for ten days or more – could treat ulcers and other internal ailments. After Burroughs's book, *The Master Cleanser*, was published in 1976, the 'lemonade diet' found widespread favour, and it has enjoyed a great resurgence in recent years, embraced by celebrities who want to lose weight quickly.

A more moderate lemon treatment for digestive troubles was adopted by a Chicago entrepreneur named Irvin Swartzberg in the early 1930s, after his doctor advised him to start each day with lemon juice and water. Swartzberg followed the doctor's orders religiously, but after a few months was so tired of squeezing lemons that he decided there must be a way around the task. Being an entrepreneur, he invented a preserved lemon juice and in 1934 marketed it to the food industry as ReaLemon. By 1941 the processed lemon juice with preservatives was being sold in grocery stores, packaged in yellow plastic bottles the size and shape of lemons.

Although the convenient ReaLemon undoubtedly cut into the fresh lemon market, Sunkist gave no indication of its existence when in 1947 an advert in the *Saturday Evening Post* urged readers to 'Keep regular the healthful way with LEMON and WATER. Most people find that the juice of a lemon in a glass of water – when taken daily first thing on arising – insures [sic] prompt normal elimination day after day', the ad read, sounding as if C. C. Teague himself had written it.

Sunkist ads continued to highlight health concerns after Hungarian biochemist Albert Szent-Györgyi isolated vitamin C in 1928. When commercial vitamin C appeared in pharmacies and grocery stores in the late 1930s, the advertisers shifted their emphasis to the *natural* source of the vitamin. Meanwhile, in 1936, Szent-Györgyi isolated another element in the lemon peel – 'citrin', a flavonoid (a type of pigment compound) – which he claimed was essential to maintain the strength of the capillaries, the body's smallest blood vessels. The element was named vitamin P for 'permeability'.

The purported contributions of vitamin P could not be proven, however, and since a lack of it did not appear to result in a deficiency disease, it never attained true vitamin status. Soon it was shown that citrus flavonoids had no therapeutic effect, and by 1938 Szent-Györgyi himself withdrew his claims for 'citrin' or vitamin P. Despite the defection, a Sunkist pamphlet from 1939, noting that lemons were a rich source of vitamin C, added that they were also 'valuable for yet another essential (vitamin P) known chemically as "citrin"'.

A longer-lasting selling point for lemons was the healthiness of vitamin C in its natural form. In the 1950s Sunkist declared that lemonade refreshed 'more thoroughly than any other summer drink' for one simple reason: 'Lemon juice replaces vitamin C and other energy-giving vitamins that warm weather takes away.'

Meyer Lemons

Frank N. Meyer – the man responsible for bringing the eponymous Meyer lemon to California – had two great passions: plants and walking. Born in Holland in 1875, as a young man he satisfied both desires by walking from Holland to Italy and Spain to see orange groves, taking only a compass to guide him. He nearly died crossing the Alps in a blizzard, a harbinger of conditions he would later face in Asia.

By the age of fourteen, Meyer was working as gardener's assistant at Amsterdam's botanical gardens, and he rose to become head gardener of the experimental gardens. He was periodically seized by an urge to travel, and when he was 22 he left for America by way of England, arriving in the USA in 1901. He found work at the US Department of Agriculture (USDA)greenhouses in Washington, DC, for a year until wanderlust overtook him again. He travelled to California and Mexico, studying plants and walking hundreds of miles across all of Mexico. After yet another trip to research plants in Cuba, he returned to the US and found work at the botanical gardens in St Louis, Missouri.

Meyer's profound interest in plants, combined with his zeal for long-distance walking, made him the perfect candidate for a job as an agricultural plant explorer to China. David Fairchild, head of the Foreign Plant Introduction Section of the USDA, invited Meyer for an interview in the summer of 1904. It was a sweltering day and Meyer was sweating so profusely that the stripes on his soaked shirt had run. 'But he sat on the edge of the chair with an eagerness and quick intelligence that won me in an instant', recalled Fairchild in his memoir. Meyer's 'evident passion for plants' as well as his stamina and love of walking deeply impressed Fairchild, for China's interior lacked roads and walking was essential there.[7]

From 1905, over the next thirteen years, Meyer made four major expeditions to Asia. He gathered, packed and sent back seeds, cuttings, scions and entomological specimens under the most difficult and rudimentary conditions. He walked thousands of miles across Asia – China, Russia, Japan, Persia, Tibet – on his mission to 'skim the earth in search of things good for man'. On the first expedition, between 1905 and 1908, he walked 1,800 miles from the Yangtze to Manchuria, wearing out three pairs of boots in a single three-month period. Walking was often treacherous, on narrow mountain trails and crumbling footpaths, across rickety bridges, through icy mountain streams and primeval forests. Meyer weathered howling dust storms and ice storms, wolves and prowling robbers. He found little rest on brick beds in smoky, vermin-infested country inns which were sometimes so cold that the ink froze in his pen.

It was all for the sake of finding useful plants, especially hardy or disease-resistant ones. 'I love this work very dearly', he wrote in a letter to Fairchild. 'I think I was born for the work I am engaged in now.'[8]

Meyer has been described as having 'curious contradictions'. He spoke fluent English, German and Dutch and could get by in four other languages, but never became fluent

Frank N. Meyer in China in 1908, the year he discovered the Meyer lemon. On the first of four expeditions, Meyer walked 1,800 miles, enduring rigorous terrain, weather and conditions.

in Chinese (impossible, he said, because of its scores of local dialects) or learned Eastern customs. He suffered spells of nervous depression, and could be alternately sociable or ill-tempered.

During his fourth expedition, in June 1918, Frank Meyer died in mysterious circumstances. He disappeared from a Japanese riverboat bound for Shanghai, and his body was later found in the Yangtze River. He was buried in Shanghai. The cause of his death was never determined.

Ultimately, Meyer's introductions of more than 2,500 hardy and disease-resistant plants from Asia transformed the landscape and agriculture of the USA. To name just a few examples, he introduced 42 soybean varieties, including the first oil-bearing soybeans, brought drought-resistant shade trees to American prairies, and advanced the development of improved peaches, apricots, plums and blight-resistant pears. But his immeasurable contributions have been largely forgotten except for a dwarf lemon tree he discovered in a Beijing courtyard in 1908 and delivered to the USDA Plant Introduction Station in Chico, California.

The ornamental *Citrus x myeri* tree is a natural hybrid of lemon and sweet orange, so it is more cold-hardy than a true lemon and has fewer thorns. It rapidly became a favourite for home yards and garden plots in California, even in those northern parts of the state that are too cold for growing ordinary lemon trees. (In the 1940s Meyer lemon trees were found to harbour a virus and had to be replaced by the 'Meyer Improved' strain developed by the University of California in the 1960s.)

The golden thin-skinned fruit has long been valued for its flowery fragrance and low-acid, sweeter juice, but its popularity with gourmet chefs soared in the early 1980s after the Chez Panisse pastry chef Lindsey Shere discovered that Meyer lemons, foraged from trees in Berkeley backyards, were sweeter and had a 'more delicate, complex perfume' than regular lemons, and were terrific in sherbets, tarts and other desserts. Before long, other chefs were demanding supplies of Meyer lemons, and wholesalers were paying foragers high prices to provide the fruit. Mike Foskett, a University of California agricultural field agent, noticed that his teenage son was making a lot of money from harvesting the neighbours' neglected trees. Recognizing the lucrative potential of Meyer lemons, Foskett quit his job, moved to the San Joaquin Valley and, along with his wife and another couple, started a company to grow, market and promote Meyer lemons and other citrus speciality fruit.

Immigrant Labourers

China had an impact on California lemons even before Frank Meyer brought his new variety of lemon to the state: California writer Carey McWilliams said the state's citrus industry would not have developed so rapidly 'had it not been for the presence of cheap and efficient Chinese laborers' in the 1870s and '80s.[9] Limoneira Ranch was fairly typical in its hiring practices. C. C. Teague supervised a crew of Chinese lemon pickers in 1893, but by the end of the decade these workers had been driven from California citrus groves by widespread anti-Chinese protests and harassment. Limoneira

Lemons arriving from the orchard were washed by machine, as in this photo from the early 1900s, before workers sorted the fruit by colour. Today's packing houses use computerized equipment for these tasks.

Picking lemons is still a tough job; pickers have to dress in heavy clothing to protect themselves from the trees' vicious thorns.

next hired Japanese men to prune and pack fruit in the early 1900s, and they continued to work in the packing houses until they were sent to detention camps during the Second World War; women workers replaced them. Mexicans comprised the next wave of immigrants, 5,000 arriving to work in the citrus industry between 1914 and 1919. Mexican nationals and Mexican Americans remain the majority of the labour force in California's lemon industry.

The work of lemon pickers hasn't changed much since 1893; it is still a tough job. Lemon trees are barbed with nasty thorns, so pickers wear thick leather gloves with canvas cuffs to protect their forearms, and layers of clothing covering every inch of skin, even in hot weather. It's a particularly brutal job in the desert regions of Arizona and California where temperatures during harvest can reach 49°C (120°F). Pickers select lemons by size, cutting the fruit from the stems with clippers. They move rapidly around the trees, climbing up and down ladders, kneeling under branches, filling the long canvas bags slung over their shoulders.

Until the mid-1980s citrus packing houses employed thousands of workers to wash lemons, sort them by size, colour and quality, and pack them into boxes. Now much of this work is automated. For every five people once employed in a citrus packing house, there is now just one – and many fewer packing houses exist. Electronic grading systems use scanners to pick out blemished lemons and sort the fruit by skin depth, shape, size and colour.

Before electronic sorting and grading systems, citrus packing houses in California employed thousands of skilled workers, mostly women.

C. C. Teague was proud that he knew every worker by name and that Limoneira provided comfortable housing for its employees right on the premises. In his memoir, *Fifty Years a Rancher*, he recounted that in his half-century at Limoneira there had been 'but one incident to mar an otherwise happy relationship with our employees'.[10] In 1941 during a campaign to unionize California citrus workers, 6,000 Mexican workers walked off the job, including many of Limoneira's 1,500 employees. Lemon growers resisted the workers' demands, and Limoneira hired Dust Bowl migrants to replace the striking workers. After five months the strike collapsed and pickers went back to work at their previous wages.

Lemon Avenue

By the middle of the twentieth century Southern California had long surpassed Italy as the world's top producer of lemons. Yet the attractive landscape along the Pacific Ocean with its salubrious climate had become too valuable for growing citrus. Lemon orchards in the Santa Barbara area were cut down and the land was sold off, parcel by parcel, in the 1950s and '60s to make way for development.

Just south of Santa Barbara, in the 'millionaire colony of Montecito',[11] former citrus ranches were transformed into playgrounds for the rich. The Johnston Fruit Company, in Montecito's foothills, became the exclusive San Ysidro Ranch hotel, a favourite of celebrities, with a restaurant in the former lemon packing house. The huge Crocker-Sperry Rancho Las Fuentes, which grew lemons from 1887, became a gated community with a golf course, tennis courts and fountains surrounded by expensive homes. The lemon packing house built by Chinese stonemasons in 1892, with its thick sandstone blocks and tall arched doorways designed to accommodate wagons of fruit, was converted to a clubhouse in 1967. The only signs of the vanished lemon culture are some potted lemon trees and bowls of fresh lemons in the lobby.

Santa Barbara area lemon acreage had declined by nearly two-thirds in 1978, when a major packing house in Carpinteria, south of Santa Barbara, was destroyed by fire. The Santa Barbara Lemon Association kept on for another decade, then ceased operations, marking the end of this area's lemon era.

Down the coast from Santa Barbara and inland, there are still miles of rich farmland, and agricultural zoning has slowed development. Around Santa Paula and other parts of Ventura County, farmers planted lima beans and walnut trees before lemons became the prime crop; now many of the lemon orchards have been chopped down for quick-profit crops such as raspberries and strawberries.

Bob Grether, a lemon grower who has farmed there for more than 60 years, has a long view on these changes in agriculture. His father, an immigrant from Germany, farmed 100 acres there from 1906, at first planting the whole farm with lima beans, then a wildly popular crop. He gradually shifted to walnut trees. Around 1960, when the walnut trees no longer produced enough to be profitable, they were replaced with lemon trees. Walnut Avenue, a road bordering Grether's 'home ranch', was named for the previous crop. 'In my lifetime, this road could have been called Lima Bean Avenue and Lemon Avenue,' Grether said, 'and after I'm gone maybe it will be called Strawberry Lane.'

The Grether family now owns 800 acres of citrus and avocado orchards, mainly lemons, and the family farming business manages and cares for more than another 2,000 acres of orchards. But elsewhere in these ideal 'lemon lands', agricultural acreage has been overtaken by tracts of black sheeting

Lemon crate label, 1930s. Most California lemons come from Ventura County, an ideal climate for growing lemons as the trees produce fruit and blossoms all year long.

punctured by strawberry plants or plastic tunnels housing raspberry canes. Growing berries is a short-term proposition, as opposed to lemon trees, which take five years before they produce and up to twenty years before a farmer knows if a planting decision was right.

The time investment, along with major expenses in land, trees and maintenance, discourages most would-be lemon farmers in Ventura County. Although lemon acreage has expanded to desert areas in Arizona, California's Coachella Valley and north of the Tehachapi Mountains into the San Joaquin Valley, lemon trees in these areas produce only one crop a year and are at greater risk of damage from wind, sun or frost.

In the twenty-first century California is no longer the world's largest supplier of lemons. Chile, Argentina, Mexico and Spain are increasingly competitive in the global marketplace, since buyers in Japan, Europe and America now demand a year-round supply of fruit. In 2003, responding to that demand, Sunkist began importing citrus from foreign sources to supplement Californian and Arizonan suppliers.

The original California lemon empire, Limoneira, still grows lemons, along with avocados, oranges and speciality crops, but is now also in the business of property development. In 2010 the company became a public stock corporation, and shortly thereafter announced that it would sever ties with Sunkist Growers.

On his Ventura County ranch, where rows of lemon trees extend to distant sunbaked slopes, Bob Grether said he had found that 'in the long run, the most consistent good thing is citrus. We're heavy on lemons and we're going to stay that way', he added. 'I'm bullish on lemons. I'm an optimist.'

7
At Home and In the World

Around the globe some of the prime lemon growing lands, especially in appealing coastal areas, have given way to housing developments or the tourist industry. The towns of Goleta, California, just north of Santa Barbara, and Menton, France, on the French-Italian Riveria, celebrate their agricultural history with lemon festivals, though lemon farming in these areas has declined severely.

Yet along the Mediterranean coast of Southern Italy, traditional lemon farming still flourishes, a healthy accompaniment to a thriving tourist economy. Some of the most valuable lemons in the world come from the Amalfi Coast. Here, since 1825, three generations of the Aceto family have tended lemon orchards on terraced hillsides above the sea, but it was only in 1992 that they organized a cooperative of Amalfi growers and gave the lemons a regional brand, 'Limone Costa d'Amalfi'. The European Union honours such lemons, along with those from the nearby Sorrentine coast, with its prestigious PGI (Protected Geogrpahical Indication) label, designating a traditionally produced regional food. This means buyers recognize their superiority, and are willing to pay accordingly.

So what makes these lemons exceptional? By many accounts it's not only the variety of lemon planted here, but also

Lemons and oranges are celebrated with huge floats at the Fête du Citron in Menton, France, on the Riviera. In the late 17th century and throughout the 18th, Menton had a 'Lemon Council' of 27 members entrusted with supervising the harvesting and selling of the crop.

Lemons and other citrus fruits are sold at the Los Angeles wholesale market and sent around the USA.

the ancient farming practices, still vibrantly alive. Amalfi Coast orchards are tiny, carefully tended jewels perched on layered shelves of earth, farmed with distinctively Old World methods. Chestnut trellises support the trees; woven straw matting, called *pagliarelle*, or black mesh netting completely covers the orchards in winter, not only protecting them from cold, wind and hail but also minimizing sunlight in order to delay ripening. Some believe that a long, slow ripening gives the lemon rind its esteemed concentrated aroma and flavour.

Amalfi lemons are pale yellow, large and well formed, with few seeds and abundant acidic juice. The rind, their most treasured asset, is sweet and intensely fragrant. A large percentage of these lemons are made into the popular local product limoncello, a concentrated lemon-rind liqueur. It takes six kilos – more than thirteen pounds – of lemon rind to make one litre of limoncello. Nearly every visitor to this region – and there are many – has sampled this liqueur, which, as Charles

Prized lemons on the Amalfi Coast are grown on terraces using Old World methods: trellises to support the trees and net coverings to protect the fruit.

Perry writes, 'explodes in your mouth with all the freshness and optimism of lemon'.[1]

Lemon Oil, Lemon Juice

The lemon's essential oils, which infuse limoncello with its lively flavour, are contained in oval sacs just below the peel's surface. Lemon oil has more than 100 chemical components, the principle one being D-limonene, which is used as a solvent.

Traditionally, in Italy and Spain, lemon rinds were hand-pressed and the oil collected in sponges, similar to ancient methods of collecting citron oil for perfume. In the latter half of the eighteenth century the most popular scents in France were made from the essential oils of citrus. 'Lemon perfume excels over all the others', wrote the French author of *Treaty on Distillation* in 1777. 'The most fashionable essences are lemon peel; it is true that their perfume is delightful.'[2]

Now lemon rinds are pressed by extraction machines in processing plants. A ton of lemons will yield ten pounds (4.5 kg) of oil. Huge truckloads of lemons roll into Sunkist's products plant, which can process 75 tons of fruit every hour into juice, pulp and lemon oil. ReaLemon is a prominent buyer of lemon juice; Coca-Cola and other beverage companies are the biggest purchasers of lemon oil for soft drinks. The clean, refreshing scent of lemon oil is used in countless products, from detergent, furniture polish and air freshener to shampoo, moisturizer and perfume.

After the juice and oil are extracted, most of the remaining peel and pulp, known as 'rag', is sold for animal feed, particularly to dairy farmers who mix the citrus with cottonseed and other feed. Cows, they say, love lemon peel.

Lemon oil's pleasant scent has strong marketing value, and it is used in countless household products.

Buying and Selling

At the age of fifteen, James Silvio, the son of Sicilian immigrants, was working as a shoeshine boy opposite the Los Angeles Produce Market. One day he walked across the street and got a job as a produce buyer. Eventually, in 1955, he started his own wholesale citrus business. His son, Joe, grew up learning about buying and selling citrus, working on weekends and school holidays with his father and eventually taking charge. For decades, Joe Silvio has started to work before dawn (as early as 1 a.m.), surrounded by stacks of boxes packed with oranges, lemons, grapefruit and limes, taking telephone orders for all grades of fruit.

Lisbon and Eureka are the two most common varieties of lemons grown in the USA, Argentina and Chile, and they are so similar that few people can tell them apart. American lemons are packed and sold according to standards of colour and appearance set by the US Department of Agriculture. Number 3 lemons are blemished but still perfectly functional for producing juice. Number 2 lemons, which cost half as much again, look nearly perfect except for small visual defects, including variations on the classic lemon shape. Then there are Number 1 lemons, costing twice as much as the Number 2s. They are large, uniformly yellow, perfectly shaped and without flaws.

Altogether, Joe Silvio sells about 1,000 40-pound (18-kg) boxes of lemons every day, with orders sent to grocery stores and restaurant suppliers across the USA, including some shipped by boat to Hawaii. Silvio buys his lemons from Sunkist as well as other citrus cooperatives. Some are imported from Chile, but most of the fresh lemons sold in the USA are grown in California – at least for now.

The 'jewel of markets worldwide' for lemons, the USA attracts imports from all those who can ship there, particularly Chile and Mexico.[3] Argentina, which has enormous lemon plantings, as of 2012 had no access to the US market because of concerns about pests and diseases, but does sell to Canada.

From year to year and season to season, the situation changes. Since 2010 South Africa has sold a new type of seedless (Eureka) lemon and Chinese lemon production has been increasing, developing into 'formidable competition' for US sellers in Asia. Meanwhile, the market in China was growing rapidly while demand in the US and Japan had declined due to the economic downturn. Traditionally, between 60 and 70 per cent of Sunkist's fresh lemons are sold to US suppliers for the restaurant business – accordingly, when restaurants suffer, so does the lemon industry.

All types of citrus, including lemon, are vulnerable to diseases that can profoundly affect world supply. From the

1930s until the 1950s a viral disease called tristeza, meaning 'sadness' in Spanish and Portuguese, spread from South America around the world, killing about 100 million citrus trees and damaging millions more. Today another killer disease threatens citrus crops around the world: Huanglongbing, or HLB for short. It's a highly infectious bacterial disease, carried by the Asian citrus psyllid, which prevents the fruit from reaching maturity, then kills the tree. There is no cure for the infected trees, and their fruit is misshapen and so bitter that it cannot be sold fresh or processed into juice. HLB, called the most devastating of all citrus diseases, has already destroyed tens of thousands of acres of citrus groves in Florida, Brazil and China. In California and other citrus-producing regions, its spread is greatly feared.

Citrus availability is also affected, albeit in a more temporary way, by weather, especially freezes. This is particularly true of the frost-sensitive lemon. For example, in the summer of 2010 a freeze vastly reduced the supply of Argentine lemons, so other lemon suppliers, such as those in California, stepped in to fill orders around the globe. As one California lemon farmer said, 'It's always someone's bad luck to make your good luck in the agriculture business.'

A Love of Lemons

No matter where they come from, lemons are so ubiquitous today that it is often only in their absence that we fully appreciate them. In the early 1800s the British clergyman Sydney Smith described the remoteness of his parish in Yorkshire as 'so far out of the way, that it was actually twelve miles from a lemon'. During the California Gold Rush, fortune seekers subsisting on diets of salted beef and hardtack suffered

This ad of 1946 advised squeezing a dozen or more lemons every two or three days, adding sugar and storing in the refrigerator, for fresh 'instant' lemonade any time.

from scurvy and were grateful to pay $1 for one lemon – the equivalent of $20 today. Britain's wartime rationing, beginning in 1940, made lemons nearly unavailable, and they were profoundly missed. As Winston Churchill arranged to meet with Franklin D. Roosevelt aboard a ship on the south coast of Newfoundland in 1941, the Americans were advised to bring foods to please the British party: ham, wine and fruit – especially lemons.

Cooks and chefs, the lemon's greatest devotees, are most apt to miss them. In 2007, after a winter freeze in California devastated a host of crops from lettuce to avocados and citrus, American chefs said the one fresh product they missed most was lemons. Cooking without lemons, as California chef Alice Waters once noted, was 'unthinkable'.

A lemon meringue pie, French lemon tart and Shaker lemon pie are but a few of the countless desserts starring lemons.

The lemon became a star of the dessert world in Europe after the mid-seventeenth century, when sugar became readily available at a reasonable cost. The British adored a rich lemon custard, which was first called a 'pudding' and later dubbed 'lemon curd', using it as both a preserve and a pie filling. The French made exquisite lemon tarts and madeleine cakes flavoured with enough lemon zest to inspire Proust. The Germans topped their lemon tarts with baroque swirls of golden-tinged meringue. The Americans embraced lemon meringue pie from the early 1800s and later adapted the recipe to employ cornflour (cornstarch), invented in the mid-1800s, to thicken the lemon filling. Unlike other fruit pies, lemon meringue could be made in any season without relying on canned goods, and it appeared often in home kitchens and diners as well as fine restaurants.

There are countless other lemon desserts, as well as savoury dishes and lemonade, which emphasize the fruit's tart punch. But it's really in its quiet, behind-the-scenes role that we depend on lemons the most. Lemons can 'cook' a ceviche of fish or shellfish without using heat, keep apples or artichokes from turning brown, or add pectin to home-made jam.

Lemon juice is a versatile ingredient that revives dull sensibilities, its brightness counteracting fishy or heavy flavours as well as cloying sweetness. Southern Italians squeeze lemon juice on just about anything: vegetables, fish, fried food, even grilled steak and lamb chops. Lemon and olive oil bind in classic salad dressings, sauces and marinades. Lemon zest adds a delicate perfume to baked goods and countless other dishes. Lemons rarely claim centre stage but rather make everything they touch taste fresher, more appealing. 'It is seasonless, sourceless, immune to fads, a commodity untouched by the shifting culinary winds', writes Amanda Hesser. 'Every cook, rich or poor, uses the fruit.'[4]

Even beyond cooking, the lemon has always had the power to rejuvenate, its fresh fragrance giving a sense of zesty vitality. In Provence the lemon is thought to confer the energy of the sun.[5] One need only scratch the surface of a lemon and breathe in its scent to understand why physicians in the Middle Ages prescribed lemon zest to ward off melancholy.

'A yellow goblet of miracles', wrote Pablo Neruda in 'Ode to the Lemon'. In the twenty-first century, the lemon that Neruda praises – 'a ray of light that was made fruit' – still evokes an age-old romance.

Recipes

Tips on Cooking with Lemons

Measuring: 4 medium lemons = approximately 1 cup (240 ml) of juice.
1 medium lemon = approximately 1 tablespoon grated peel.

Lemon juice: Lemons should be room temperature or warmer. Rolling a lemon firmly on the countertop with your palm causes the membranes inside to break down, releasing more juice.

Cooking: Use nonreactive cookware with lemon juice, avoiding aluminium, uncoated cast iron or copper. It's best to add lemon juice to dishes after cooking to retain the vitamin C. Lemon juice tenderizes meat so is excellent in marinades. Perk up wilted lettuce or tired vegetables by soaking them in a bowl of cold water with a teaspoon of lemon juice for 30 minutes. Lemon juice can also prevent cut fruits or artichokes from oxidizing, or turning brown.

Lemon zest: Use unwaxed or organic lemons for zest, or blanch lemons in boiling water for a minute to loosen the wax and scrub the skin well before grating. A rasp-style grater results in finely grated zest; a lemon zester produces slightly longer threads. Be sure to grate only the yellow rind, not the white pith beneath.

Preserving juice and zest: Lemon juice can be frozen in small containers or ice-cube trays, which can then be added to lemonade or thawed for a recipe. Lemon zest can also be frozen, wrapped in small packets of cling film (plastic wrap) or aluminium foil. For lemon sugar (for baking), add lemon peel to a jar of sugar.

Historic Recipes

Preserved Lemons

from Ibn Jumay, *On Lemon, Its Drinking and Use* (twelfth century),
reprinted Samuel Tolkowsky, *Hesperides: A History of the Culture and Use of Citrus Fruits* (London, 1938)

Take lemons that are fully ripe and of bright yellow color; cut them open without severing the two halves and introduce plenty of fine salt into the split; place the fruits thus prepared in a glass vessel having a wide opening and pour over them more lemon juice until they are completely submerged; now close the vessel and seal it with wax and let it stand for a fortnight in the sun, after which store it away for at least forty days; but if you wait still longer than this before eating them, their taste and fragrance will be still more delicious and their action in stimulating the appetite will be stronger.

To Make a Lemon Pudding

from Hannah Glasse, *The Art of Cookery Made Plain and Easy* (1747)

Versions of lemon pudding, which appeared in European cookbooks from the mid-1700s, were forerunners of lemon pies. 'Naples biscuits' were small sponge cakes similar to sponge fingers (ladyfingers).

Grate the outside rind of two clear lemons; then grate two Naples biscuits and mix with the grated peel, and add to it three quarters of a pound of white sugar, twelve yolks of eggs and half the whites, three quarters of a pound of melted butter, half a pint of thick cream; mix all well together; lay a puff paste all over the dish, pour the ingredients in and bake it. An hour will bake it.

Shaker Lemon Pie

Start this pie the day before you want to eat it, as the lemons need time to macerate in the sugar. Meyer lemons, with thinner skins, require less time; regular lemons require longer.

pastry dough for a 9-inch (20-cm) double-crust pie, refrigerated
2 large or 4 small lemons, Meyer or regular
1¾ cups (275 g) sugar
¼ teaspoon salt
4 eggs
4 tablespoons butter, melted
3 tablespoons plain (all-purpose) flour

Thoroughly wash the lemons; blanch for one minute in boiling water; drain and dry. Cut off the ends of each lemon and cut into paper-thin slices, removing the seeds. Put the lemon slices in a bowl and toss with the sugar and salt. Cover and set aside at room temperature for 24 hours or longer.

Roll out half the dough to a 12-inch (30-cm) circle; fit into a 9-inch (20-cm) pie pan and trim, leaving a ½-inch (1.5-cm) overhang, and refrigerate for 30 minutes. Preheat the oven to 425°F / 220°C.

Whisk the eggs and beat in the melted butter; remove ½ cup of this mixture and add the flour to it, stirring till smooth, then incorporate it back into the egg-butter mixture, and add the mixture to the macerated lemons. Pour into prepared pie shell.

Roll the remaining dough into a 12-inch (30-cm) round, drape it over the filling and trim, leaving a 1-inch (2.5-cm) overhang. Fold the overhang under the bottom crust, pressing the edge to seal it, and crimp the edge. Cut slits in the top for steam vents, and bake the pie for 25 minutes. Reduce temperature to 350°F / 180°C and bake for 20 to 25 minutes more, or until the crust is golden. Let the pie cool on a rack. Serve at room temperature.

Savoury Favourites

Avgolemono – Greek Egg-lemon Soup

This Greek speciality is also served in the Middle East and parts of North Africa.)

4 cups (900 ml) chicken broth
⅓ cup (65 g) uncooked white rice
2 eggs
¼ cup (50 ml) lemon juice
salt, pepper and cayenne to taste

Bring the stock to a boil in a large saucepan and add the rice. Cook until rice is just cooked through, about 17 minutes. Meanwhile, in a medium bowl, whisk the eggs and lemon juice until smooth. Ladle half a cup of the hot stock into the egg mixture, whisking constantly. Slowly pour the mixture back into the remaining stock, whisking constantly.

Continue to cook and stir over low heat until soup becomes opaque and slightly thickened, a few minutes. Do not let it boil or the eggs will scramble.

Season with salt, pepper and cayenne, if you wish. Serve the soup hot, garnished with chopped parsley or fresh mint and lemon slices.

Slow-roast Chicken with Garlic and Lemons

A classic roast chicken calls for stuffing the chicken cavity with one or two lemons, pricked with a fork to let out the juices. This alternative recipe roasts cut lemons, skin and all, right alongside the chicken pieces, for about 2½ hours. Add a cup (180 g) of pitted green olives for a Moroccan flavour.

> 2 lb (900 g) boneless chicken thighs, skin removed
> 1 head of garlic, separated into cloves
> 2 large Meyer or regular lemons
> 3 tablespoons olive oil
> 1–2 tablespoons fresh thyme leaves or rosemary
> salt and pepper
> ¾ cup (150 ml) white wine
> ¼ cup (50 ml) lemon juice

Place the chicken in a Dutch oven or casserole, along with the cloves of garlic, fresh thyme or rosemary and the 2 lemons, cut in half vertically and cut into slices, seeds removed.

Salt and pepper the chicken, pour olive oil over everything and mix so the oil coats everything. Pour the white wine over all and cover with a lid or aluminium foil. Put in preheated oven to cook for 2 hours at 300°F/150°C.

Turn the oven to 400°F/200°C, add the lemon juice and roast for another 15 to 20 minutes. Serve over rice, potatoes or pasta. Serves 4 or more

Lemon Basil Linguine

You could use rosemary or other herbs in place of basil, or add greens (kale or chard, for example) sautéed with minced garlic to the dish. It's also very good with a tablespoon of capers added at the same time as the cheese.

> ½ lb (225 g) linguine
> 1 tablespoon grated lemon zest
> ¼ cup (50 ml) lemon juice
> ¼ cup (50 ml) olive oil
> ¼ to ½ cup (25 to 50 g) grated Parmigiano or Pecorino cheese

handful of basil leaves, torn into small pieces
salt and pepper

Bring a big pot of salted water to the boil and cook linguine until done, al dente (7 or 8 minutes). Meanwhile, gently warm the olive oil, lemon juice and lemon zest in a small pan and whisk till emulsified; then add the torn basil and cheese and whisk again. Add salt and pepper to taste.

Drain linguine and toss together with sauce until each strand is coated evenly. Serve immediately.

Serves 2

Lemon Drinks, Desserts and Marmalade

Zesty Lemonade

For a simple lemonade, stir sugar into a glass or pitcher of water and add freshly squeezed lemon juice to taste. This version extracts the delicious flavour of zest as well.

1 cup (200 g) sugar
3 cups (675 ml) water
1 cup (225 ml) lemon juice
1 whole lemon, cut into thin slices

Juice the lemons, setting aside the empty skins. Boil 2 cups (450 ml) of the water with the sugar in a saucepan, stirring until the sugar is dissolved. Take the saucepan off the heat, add the lemon skins and cover for 20 minutes.

Remove the rinds, squeezing out any liquid into the pan. Pour the syrup into a pitcher and add the remaining water, lemon juice and lemon slices. Taste and add more water if you like, but remember your lemonade will be diluted with ice.

Chill and serve in glasses filled with ice cubes, putting a slice of lemon in each glass.

To flavour lemonade, steep sprigs of mint or rosemary or slices of ginger; add a bit of rose water; mix in apricot or mango nectar, puréed watermelon or berries – or almost any combination of fruits, herbs and spices you like.

Lemon Curd

This is a foolproof method – as long as you keep stirring and don't let it boil.

¾ to 1 cup (150 to 200 g) sugar, depending on how tart or sweet you like it
6 tablespoons butter, softened
2 large eggs
2 large egg yolks
⅔ cup (150 ml) fresh lemon juice
1 tablespoon grated lemon zest

Cream the sugar and butter together using an electric mixer until smooth, then add the eggs and egg yolks and beat again. Mix in the lemon juice. The mixture will look curdled, but don't worry – it will come back together when heated.

Put the mixture in a medium saucepan and heat over moderately low heat, stirring constantly. Do not let the mixture boil. Cook until thickened – when the mixture coats the back of a wooden spoon. This will take about 15 to 20 minutes.

Take the mixture off the heat and stir in the lemon zest. Let the curd cool, stirring every once in a while to prevent a skin from forming. Refrigerate in a covered container until ready to use.

French Lemon Tart

This pastry shell is an easy pat-in-the-pan version, which is filled with the lemon curd above. You may want to double the curd recipe for a more generous amount of filling.

8 tablespoons unsalted butter, melted and cooled
¼ teaspoon plus ⅛ teaspoon vanilla essence
1 tablespoon grated lemon zest
¼ cup (50 g) icing (confectioner's) sugar
pinch of salt
1 ¼ cup (175 g) plus 1 tablespoon plain (all-purpose) flour

Preheat oven to 350°F / 180°C. Butter the sides and bottom of a 9-inch tart pan.

In a medium bowl, combine the butter, vanilla, sugar and salt. Add enough flour to form a smooth, soft dough. Place the dough in the centre of the tart pan and press evenly on bottom and sides.

Place in the centre of the oven and bake until the dough is firm and lightly browned, 12 to 15 minutes. Remove from the oven and let it cool at least 10 minutes before filling.

Fill the tart with lemon curd and put the tart in the middle of an oven preheated to 325°F / 170°C. Bake for 15 minutes. Remove to a wire rack and let cool. Refrigerate well before serving.

Meyer Lemon Marmalade

6 Meyer lemons, medium size (about 1 ½ lb (680 g))
4 cups (900 ml) water
4 cups (800 g) sugar

Cut the lemons in half crosswise and remove the seeds. Put the seeds in a square of doubled cheesecloth and tie it into a bag using string. Quarter each lemon half and thinly slice. Place the lemons and bag of seeds with the water in a 5-quart (5-litre) nonreactive heavy pot and let the mixture stand, covered, at room temperature for 24 hours.

Bring the lemon mixture to a boil over moderate heat. Reduce heat and simmer, uncovered, until reduced to 4 cups (900 ml), about 45 minutes. Stir in the sugar and boil over moderate heat, stirring occasionally and skimming off any foam, until a teaspoon of mixture dropped on a cold plate gels (or reaches 212°F/100°C), about 30 minutes.

Ladle the hot marmalade into sterilized jars, filling to within ¼ inch (½ cm) of top. Wipe the rims with a dampened cloth and seal the jars with lids. If you're going to keep the marmalade in the refrigerator, you can skip the next step.

Put the jars in a water-bath canner, adding enough hot water to cover the jars by 1 inch (2.5 cm). Bring water to a boil and boil jars for 5 minutes. Using tongs, transfer the jars to a rack and cool completely.

The marmalade keeps, stored in a cool, dark place, for up to a year. But it's so good that it's very unlikely to be around that long.

For more recipes, see http://tobysonneman.wordpress.com

References

1 Origins and Obsessions

1 Larry Luxner, 'Sweet Mystery', *Americas*, XLV/2 (1993), pp. 2–3.
2 Samuel Tolkowsky, *Hesperides: A History of the Culture and Use of Citrus Fruits* (London, 1938), p. 19.
3 Alan Davidson, *The Oxford Companion to Food* (Oxford, 1999), p. 187.
4 Eric Isaac and Rael Isaac, 'A Goodly Tree: Sacred and Profane History', *Commentary Magazine* (October 1958), pp. 300–7.
5 Sholom Aleichem, 'The Esrog', in *Holiday Tales of Sholom Aleichem*, selected and trans. Aliza Shevrin (New York, 1979), p. 76.
6 Michael Strassfeld, *The Jewish Holidays: A Guide and Commentary* (New York, 1985), p. 131.
7 Isaac and Isaac, 'A Goodly Tree', p. 307.

2 Sicily: Arab Mediterranean

1 Andrew M. Watson, 'The Arab Agricultural Revolution and its Diffusion, 700–1100', *Journal of Economic History* (March 1974), pp. 8–35.
2 Clifford Wright, *Cucina Paradiso: The Heavenly Food of Sicily* (New York, 1992), p. 76. For more on Sicilians'

love of lemons see Mary Taylor Simeti, *Pomp and
Sustenance: Twenty-five Centuries of Sicilian Food* (New
York, 1990), p. 63.

3 Charles Perry, trans., *A Baghdad Cookery Book* (London,
2005), pp. 37–8.

4 S. D. Goitein, *A Mediterranean Society: The Jewish Communities
of the Arab World as Portrayed in the Documents of the Cairo
Geniza*, vol. IV (Berkeley, CA, 1967), pp. 230–31.

5 Wright, *Cucina Paradiso*, p. 145.

6 Consoli is the author of *Sicilia: Cucina del Sole* (Catania,
1986), a two-volume classic of Sicilian cooking, and runs
a cooking school, Cucina del Sole, in Viagrande, Sicily.

7 Detailed in Elizabeth David, *Harvest of the Cold Months:
The Social History of Ice and Ices* (New York, 1994).

8 Samuel Tolkowsky, *Hesperides: A History of the Culture and
Use of Citrus Fruits* (London, 1938), p. 134.

9 Charles Perry, 'Preserved Lemons', *Petits Propos Culinaires*,
50 (August 1995), p. 23 and 'Sleeping Beauties', *Los Angeles
Times*, 30 March 1995, p. 19.

10 Quoted in Tolkowsky, *Hesperides*, p. 133.

3 Exotic Treasure

1 Ivan Day, 'The Art of Confectionery' (1993), at www.
historicfood.com.

2 Alan Davidson, *The Oxford Companion to Food* (Oxford,
1999), p. 449.

3 J. W. Goethe, trans. W. H. Auden and Elizabeth Mayer,
Italian Journey (1786–1788) (London, 1970), p. 43.

4 The Lemon Cure

1 Stephen R. Brown, *Scurvy: How a Surgeon, a Mariner, and a
Gentleman Solved the Greatest Medical Mystery of the Age of Sail*
(New York, 2003), p. 3.

2 Ibid., p. 37.
3 Kenneth J. Carpenter, *The History of Scurvy and Vitamin C* (Cambridge, 1986), pp. 15–17.
4 An exception was Lancaster's 1601 lemon juice experiment. The juice was preserved by a secret method.

5 Lemonade

1 S. D. Goitein, *A Mediterranean Society: The Jewish Communities of the Arab World as Portrayed in the Documents of the Cairo Geniza*, vol. I (Berkeley, CA, 1967), p. 420.
2 Catherine Merlo, *Heritage of Gold: The First 100 Years of Sunkist Growers, Inc., 1893–1993* (Sherman Oaks, CA, 1993), p. 31.

6 To and From the Golden State

1 G. W. Garcelon, *Citrus Fruits: Fifteen Years with the Lemon* (Sacramento, CA, 1891), p. 6.
2 Edward James Wickson, *The California Fruits and How to Grow Them* (San Francisco, CA, 1889), p. 457.
3 Quoted in Richard G. Lillard, 'Agricultural Statesman: Charles C. Teague of Santa Paula', *California History* (March 1986), p. 5.
4 Charles Collins Teague, *10 Talks on Citrus Marketing: A Series of Radio Broadcasts* (Los Angeles, CA, 1939).
5 Ibid.
6 Lillard, 'Agricultural Statesman', p. 16.
7 David Fairchild, *The World Was My Garden: Travels of a Plant Explorer* (New York, 1941), p. 315.
8 Quoted in Isabel Shipley Cunningham, *Frank N. Meyer: Plant Hunter in Asia* (Ames, IA, 1984), p. 129.
9 Carey McWilliams, *Southern California Country: An Island on the Land* (New York, 1946), pp. 89–90.
10 Charles Collins Teague, *Fifty Years a Rancher* (Los Angeles, CA, 1944), p. 148.

11 Federal Writers Project, *California: A Guide to the Golden State* (New York, 1939), p. 393.

7 At Home and In the World

1 Charles Perry, 'Taste of a Thousand Lemons', *Los Angeles Times*, 8 September 2004.

2 Quoted in Samuel Tolkowsky, *Hesperides: A History of the Culture and Use of Citrus Fruits* (London, 1938), p. 280.

3 Email interviews with John Eliot, Exchange/Business manager of Saticoy Lemon Association, 21 October 2010 and 2 March 2012. Eliot provided the quote and information in this and the subsequent paragraph.

4 Amanda Hesser, 'Citrus Maximus', *New York Times Magazine*, 6 November 2005, pp. 95–6.

5 Patricia Wells, *Patricia Wells at Home in Provence* (New York, 1996), p. 297.

Select Bibliography

Belknap, Michael R., 'The Era of the Lemon: A History of
Santa Paula, California', *California Historical Society Quarterly*,
XLVII (San Francisco, CA, 1968)

Brown, Stephen R., *Scurvy: How a Surgeon, a Mariner, and a
Gentleman Solved the Greatest Medical Mystery of the Age of Sail*
(New York, 2003)

Carpenter, Kenneth J., *The History of Scurvy and Vitamin C*
(Cambridge, 1988)

Cunningham, Isabel Shipley, *Frank N. Meyer: Plant Hunter in Asia*
(Ames, IA, 1984)

David, Elizabeth, *Harvest of the Cold Months: The Social History of
Ice and Ices* (New York, 1994)

Isaac, Eric, and Rael Isaac, 'A Goodly Tree: Sacred and
Profane History', *Commentary Magazine* (October 1958),
pp. 300–7

Laszlo, Pierre, *Citrus: A History* (Chicago, IL, 2007)

Lillard, Richard G., 'Agricultural Statesman: Charles C. Teague
of Santa Paula', *California History* (March 1986)

McWilliams, Carey, *Southern California Country: An Island on the
Land* (New York, 1946)

McPhee, John, *Oranges* (New York, 1966)

Merlo, Catherine, *Heritage of Gold: The First 100 Years of Sunkist
Growers, Inc., 1893–1993* (Los Angeles, CA, 1993)

Norwich, John Julius, *The Normans in Sicily: The Normans in the
South, 1016–1130, and the Kingdom in the Sun, 1130–1194* (London,
1992)

Reuther, Walter, Herbert John Webber and Leon Dexter
    Batchelor, *The Citrus Industry*, vol. 1 (Berkeley, CA, 1967)
    available online at http://library.ucr.edu
Simeti, Mary Taylor, *Pomp and Sustenance: Twenty-five Centuries of
    Sicilian Food* (New York, 1990)
Smith, Dennis Mack, *A History of Sicily: Medieval Sicily, 800–1713*
    (New York, 1968)
Sonneman, Toby, 'The Saga of the Citron', *Reform Judaism
    Magazine* (Fall 2003)
Teague, Charles Collins, *Fifty Years a Rancher* (Los Angeles, CA,
    1944)
Tolkowsky, Samuel, *Hesperides: A History of the Culture and Use of
    Citrus Fruits* (London, 1938)
Visser, Margaret, *Much Depends on Dinner: The Extraordinary
    Allure and Obsessions, Perils and Taboos of an Ordinary Meal*
    (New York, 1986)
Watson, Andrew M., 'The Arab Agricultural Revolution and Its
    Diffusion, 700–1100', *Journal of Economic History* (March
    1974), pp. 8–35
Woods, May, and Arete Warren, *Glass Houses: A History of
    Greenhouses, Orangeries and Conservatories* (New York, 1988)
Wright, Clifford, *A Mediterranean Feast: The Story of the Birth of the
    Celebrated Cuisines of the Mediterranean, from the Merchants of
    Venice to the Barbary Corsairs* (New York, 1999)

Websites and Associations

Amalfi Citrus-Fruit Processing Co-operative
http://cata.amalfi.it/history.htm

Citrus Clonal Protection Program (University of California)
http://ccpp.ucr.edu

Citrus Variety Collection (University of California)
www.citrusvariety.ucr.edu

The Citrus Label Gallery
www.citruslabelgallery.com

Citrus Label Society
www.citruslabelsociety.com

Home Citrus Growers
www.homecitrusgrowers.co.uk

Lemon festival in Menton, France
www.feteducitron.com

Saticoy Lemon Association
www.saticoylemon.com

Sunkist
www.sunkist.com

Tips on cooking with lemons and lemon recipes from the author
http://tobysonneman.wordpress.com

Acknowledgements

I would like to thank the citrus experts who offered me guidance, assistance and sources to help me understand nearly every aspect of the lemon, particularly John Eliot of Saticoy Lemon Association, fruit aficionado David Karp, horticulture expert Lance Walheim, and Tracy Kahn and the late Bill Bitters, curators of the Citrus Variety Collection at UC Riverside.

For citrus history, I owe a huge debt – as does anyone who writes about this subject – to Samuel Tolkowsky, whose book *Hesperides: A History of the Culture and Use of Citrus Fruits* (1938) is a comprehensive treasury of everything written or observed about citrus in the previous millennium. I am also grateful to those who helped me in my journeys to the lemon lands, which added so much more than I could ever have learned from texts. Special thanks go to Whatcom Community College for a travel grant, to Centrum, for its artist residency programme, to the extraordinary Eleonora Consoli for her delicious lessons in Sicilian history and cuisine, and to Mary Taylor Simeti for assisting with an early version of the chapter on Sicily.

I deeply appreciate all the lemon growers and others involved with lemons who gave enlightening and entertaining tours through their orchards or workplaces, particularly Mike and Barbara Foskett, Mario DiPaolo, Joe Silvio, Craig Armstrong, Gary Ball, John Borchard, Ken Doty, Jim Finch, Link Leavens, the Brokaw family and the people of Limoneira Company. I especially cherish the friendship of Bob and Sally Grether and their wonderful annual lemon orchard tours; and the friendship of John and Shirley

Kirkpatrick, who not only educated me about the intricacies of citron growing for the religious market but also send me an *etrog* every autumn for the Jewish holiday.

I'm grateful to many for encouragement and insight about turning my long lemon odyssey into a book. Thanks especially to Paul Wilderson, to my grown children Zak and Aviva Steigmeyer, to Claire Smith of Sunkist and to Andy Smith and Michael Leaman of Reaktion Books. I particularly appreciate Cathy Mihalik's lively interest, companionship and willingness to drive through twisting mountain tunnels to see the lemon houses of Lake Garda. And I am profoundly grateful to my partner Steve Sanger who has lived with my lemon obsession for nearly a decade, tirelessly accompanying me on interviews and trips to lemon orchards from Southern California to Sicily, reading innumerable versions of my manuscript with a reporter's clear eye, and readily eating enough lemon-flavoured dishes to last a lifetime. Through it all, his support of the lemon project has sustained me.

Photo Acknowledgements

The author and the publishers wish to express their thanks to the below sources of illustrative material and/or permission to reproduce it:

Archbishop chateau in Krom íž, Czech Republic: pp. 12, 45, 47, 49, 50, 51, 52; © Trustees of the British Museum: pp. 26, 65, 71; Comune di Limone sul Garda, Italy: pp. 53, 55; Goleta Valley Historical Society: p. 101; Istockphoto: p. 6 (Ekspansio); Library of Congress: pp. 30, 35; Limoneira Company: pp. 85, 99; McClelland Collection: p. 71; Cathy Mihalik, p. 77; National Agricultural Library, Special Collections: p. 97; National Library of Medicine, Bethesda, Maryland: p. 60; Polo Museale, Florence: p. 43; Reading Public Museum, Reading, Pennsylvania: p. 73; Rijksmuseum, Amsterdam: p. 42; S. Jim Campos Collection: pp. 84, 86, 87, 88; Nicolas Sartore, photographer, Office de Tourisme Menton (www. flickr.com/photos/tourisme-menton), p. 108; Sunkist Growers: pp. 80, 89, 91,92, 113; Victoria & Albert Museum, London: pp. 14, 17, 39.

Index

italic numbers refer to illustrations; **bold** to recipes